S0-ACB-706

CHICAGO PUBLIC LIBRARY
HAROLD WASHINGTON LIBRARY CENTER
R0021728760

Printing in Colonial Spanish America

By
Lawrence S. Thompson

ARCHON BOOKS
THE SHOE STRING PRESS, INC.
HAMDEN, CONNECTICUT
LONDON, ENGLAND

Library of Congress Catalog Card No: 62-20454
Printed in the United States of America

To

Algernon Smith Dickson Thompson

1922-1962

CONTENTS

ILLUSTRATIONS

Note: The brief "titles" used above are for identification only. Please see pages indicated for full information.

INTRODUCTION

Anglo-Saxon Americans are likely to think of their pioneer era as the most colorful chapter in the history of the New World. Students of Spanish-American history know better. More than a century before Jamestown in Virginia was settled, a Spanish colony was firmly established in Santo Domingo. The fabulous conquests of Cortez in Mexico and of Pizarro in Peru have few parallels north of the Río Bravo del Norte, or indeed, anywhere in the world. Even the early history of what is now the United States was enriched immensely by the explorations of Coronado, Núñez Cabeza de Vaca, and Ponce de León, although they never found the Seven Cities of Cibola or the Fountain of Youth. The heroic story of the Jesuits and their *reducciones* cannot be matched even by the great exploits of other members of the Company of Jesus in Canada and the Mississippi Valley. The riches of the New World provided a source of hard money for four centuries of Europeans, and it is little wonder that the English freebooter's eyes gleamed when he thought of the rich galleons sailing with bullion from Puerto Bello to the peninsula.

There were other more sober realities in Spanish America that presented the gravest obstacles to the advance of culture. There were vast distances that staggered the imagination, mountains and rivers more formidable than any in Europe or North America. The four great viceroyalties of New Spain, New Granada, Perú, and Buenos Aires were separated by natural barriers that have not yet fully yielded either to the railroad or to the paved highway. The indigenous population has never been fully absorbed, from a cultural standpoint. The Church of Rome held a firm grip on all moral and social life, and many governmental functions were in the hands of friars. Still, the friar and the lawyer represented a cultural tradition in Spanish America totally antithetical to the heritage of the boorish, unlettered conquistador, the alter ego of the Kentucky alligator-horse.

The metropolis was stiff-necked and uncomprehending, and viceroys and other officials were not always competent or sympathetic with their people. The Hapsburg and Bourbon monarchs were even more inept in their colonial policy than were the Stuarts and the Hanoverians. When the revolutions finally broke out in Hispanic America, they came with a terrible violence. Universities and printing presses, already established for two and a half centuries, generally stood in the ranks of the insurgents, but they represented a tradition older and totally different from that which prevailed along the North Atlantic littoral. There had been no Zenger and no Franklin south of the Tropic of Cancer to stimulate printing presses with controversial literature. The newspaper press was relatively insignificant in comparison with that of Anglo-Saxon America. Nevertheless, the colonial printers of Spanish America had developed traditions that had special meaning for the civilization they served, and that civilization would have been infinitely poorer without these traditions.

Chapter I

THE BEGINNING OF PRINTING IN MEXICO

The origins of printing in Mexico have been shrouded in almost as much mystery as the first printing in Europe; and, particularly in recent years, there have been controversies as violent as any that ever raged between Mainz and Haarlem. We know that the ecclesiastical authorities in Mexico felt an urgent need for multiple copies of basic religious works to serve the needs of Spanish friars zealous to win hundreds of thousands of Indian souls for the Church of Rome; but we are by no means certain who was the first printer to implement this fundamental aspect of Spanish imperial policy.

Heated arguments on the subject have developed in the present decade. In March 1953 the distinguished Spanish bibliographer Francisco Vindel published a little book entitled El primer libro impreso en América fué para El Rezo del Santo Rosario (Méjico, 1532-34). It contained a facsimile of the work he discovered and his reasons for believing it to have been printed from type from the shop of Juan Varela of Seville, on a small press for printing playing cards sent over to Mexico with Juan's son, Pedro, in 1531. Three eminent members of the Academia Mexicana de Historia, Juan B. Iguíniz, Alberto María Carreño, and Francisco Gómez de Orozco, made a highly critical examination of Vindel's thesis, and their conclusions were printed in the first number of the Academy's Memorias for 1954. Their only agreement with Vindel was that the little work was "indudablemente de la primera mitad del siglo XVI". Vindel denied the position of the Mexican bibliographers rather indignantly in an eight-page Replica en "Carta abierta" issued in Madrid on 10 May 1954, summarizing his attitude toward the Mexicans in the words "¡¡¡¡Un libro que no han visto!!!!"
No further conclusive evidence has been offered to identify the place, printer, and date of the little book discovered by

Vindel. As late as 1961 the book could be inspected in an antiquarian bookstore near the Puerta del Sol.

The greatest of all Spanish-American bibliographers, José Toribio Medina, believed that one Esteban Martín was the first printer in Mexico, and that he was at work from 1535 to 1538. The supporters of the Martín thesis allege that he printed the *Escala spiritual* of San Juan Climaco, but there is no extant copy of this work or anything else printed by Martín. A key document supporting the claims for Martín is a memorial from Archbishop Juan de Zumárraga to the emperor, under the date of 6 May 1538: "Poco se puede adelantar en lo de la imprenta por la carestía del papel, que esto dificulta las muchas obras que acá estan aparejadas y otras que habrán de nuevo darse a la estampa, pues que se carece de las más necesarias, y de allá son pocas las que vienen." Thus a printer must have been in Mexico in 1538. In the *Actas de Cabildo* of the municipal archives of Mexico City for 5 September 1539 it is recorded that one Esteban Martín was admitted to citizenship. Medina offers much evidence to support his thesis that Martín was the first printer in the Americas, but not all Hispanic-American bibliographers have agreed with him.

The first Mexican printer whom we can identify with absolute certainty and whose work survives is Juan Pablos, or Giovanni Paoli, a native of Brescia. He left Spain in June 1539 after rather interesting negotiations by Zumárraga and Viceroy Don Antonio de Mendoza with a leading Seville printer, Juan Cromberger. Eager to provide religious instruction for native Mexicans, Zumárraga had arranged with Cromberger to print a catechism in Nahuatl, but Cromberger decided that the job could be done more easily by a printer resident in Mexico. Accordingly, on 12 June 1539 Cromberger entered into a contract with Pablos which contained many interesting details. The agreement was to run for ten years. Cromberger would pay transportation for Pablos, his wife, his pressman (Gil Barbero), and a Negro slave, and for freight charges on the press and printing supplies. Pablos was to print 3,000 sheets a day ("tres mill pliegos," a fantastically high number for a single press), and he could have none of the income from the press beyond what was needed for bare living expenses. Pablos could engage in no other business, and he was to act as retail sales agent for his principal, but without commission on such sales. Barbero was to receive a salary of five and a half ducats per month. After ten years, all expenses, including transportation, wages, living costs, and depreciation of equipment were to be deducted from the profits, and Pablos was to receive one-fifth of the net profits. Pablos was bound to melt down old type rather than to sell it so as not to encourage competition by other printers, and all publications were to bear the imprint "en casa de Juan Cromberger". It is of some interest to note, in view of the claims for Martín as Mexico's prototypographer, that Pablos and his group did not arrive in Mexico City until September 1539, and that he was not admitted to citizenship until 17 February 1542.

Pablos went to work immediately in the service of Archbishop Zumárraga and his pious objectives. In the Cartas de Indias (1877) there is a description of a Breve y mas compendiosa doctrina christiana en lengua mexicana y castellana, que contiene las cosas mas necesarias de nuestra sancta fe catholica, para aprovechamiento destos indios naturales y salvacion de sus animas. In spite of the most diligent searches by Medina, García Icazbalceta, and other Mexican bibliographers, no trace of this precious little quarto of twelve leaves has been found. On 13 December 1540 Pablos issued a Manual de Adultos. The three surviving pages, now in the Biblioteca Nacional in Madrid, are reproduced in facsimile in García Icazbalceta's Bibliografía mexicana del siglo XVI (2d ed., 1954). The last sheet, containing a "fe de erratas", has a final correction relating to the recto of leaf 36, thus indicating that the book was one of relatively substantial proportions. The third known production of Pablos is the Relacion del espantable terremoto que agora nueuamente ha acontecido en la cibdad de Guatimala (1541), four quarto

Christophorus Cabrera Burgensis ad lectorem sacri baptisimi ministrū: Dicolon Icastichon.

Si paucis pnosse cupis: ueneráde sacerdos:
Ut baptizari quilibet Indus habet:
Quae qꝫ pꝰ dbēt ceu parua elemēta doceri:
Quicqd adultus iners scire tenetur itē:
Quaeqꝫ sient pscis pribꝰ sancita: p orbem
Ut foret ad ritū tinctꝰ adultus aqua:
Ut ne dspiciat (fors) tā sublime Charisma
Indulus ignarus terqꝫ quaterqꝫ miser:
Hūc mãibꝰ vsa: tere: plege: dilige librum:
Nil ninꝰ obscurū: nil magis est nitidum.
Siplicit docteqꝫ dedit modo Vascꝰ acutꝰ
Addo Quiroga meꝰ psul abunde pius.
Sigula ppēdens nihil ide reqrere possis:
Si placet oē legas ordine dispositum.
Ne videare (caue) sacris ignauus abuti:
Sis decet aduigilās: mittito desidiam.
Nēpe bonū nihil ūqꝫ fecerit oscitabūdus.
Difficile est pulchrū: dictitat Antiqtas.
Sed satis ē: qd me remorar pluribꝰ inqs.
Sit satis: & facias quod precor: atqꝫ uale.

Recto of first leaf of Manual de Adultos, issued by Juan Pablos on 13 December 1540, the first surviving Mexican imprint.

Doctrina breue muy p-
uechosa delas cosas q̃ perte-
cen ala fe catholica y a nr̃a cri
stiandad en estilo llano pa co-
mũ intelligẽcia. Cõpuesta por
el. Reuerẽdissimo. S. dõ fray
Juã çumarraga primer obpo
d Mexico. Del cõsejo d su ma
gestad. Impssa ẽla misma ciudad d Mexico por su mãdado
y a su costa. Año d M.dxliij.

Title-page of *Doctrina breve*, the first major work printed by Juan Pablos (1543).

Tripartito del
Christianissimo y consolato-
rio doctor Juan Gerson de
doctrina Christiana: a qual-
quiera muy ꝓuechosa. Tra-
duzido de latin en lẽgua Cas
tellana para el biẽ d' muchos
necessario. Impresso en Mexico: en casa de Juan cromberger. Por mãdado y a costa del. R. S. obispo dela mes
ma ciudad Fray Juã çumar
raga. Reuisto y examinado
por su mandado.
Año de. M. d. xliiij.

Title-page of Juan Pablos' edition of Johannes Gerson's Tripartito (1544).

leaves referring to the destructive Guatemalan earthquake of 10-11 September 1541. The fourth book printed by Pablos is his first large work, the Doctrina breve muy provechosa de las cosas que pertenecen a la fe catholica y a nuestra cristianidad (1543), a volume in eighty-four leaves of which several good copies have survived. A complete reproduction, The Doctrina breve in Facsimile, was published in 1928 as number 10 in the "Monograph Series" of the United States Catholic Historical Society.

Pablos became the sole proprietor of the press in 1547, and his total production until his death in 1560 consisted of thirty-seven known titles, most of them religious works. Many of his books attained a relatively high standard of typographical achievement. In 1544 he printed an edition of Johannes Gerson's Tripartito, the first book printed in the Americas to be illustrated with a full-page wood engraving. Another first for Pablos is the Ordenanças y copilacion de leyes (1548), the first collection of laws printed in the New World. In 1556 Pablos issued the first American arithmetic and algebra, the Sumario compendioso de las quentas de plata y oro que en los reynos del Piru son necesarias a los mercaderes by Fray Juan Díez; in the next year he brought out a monument in the history of American sciences, Fray Alonso de la Vera Cruz' Phisica speculatio. Parenthetically, it should be noted that the opening of the University of Mexico in 1553 (founded in 1551) may be considered accountable for much of the strong interest in science in sixteenth century Mexico. Francisco Bravo's Opera medicinelia (Mexico, Pedro Ocharte, 1570), Alonso Lopez de Hinojoso's Svmma, y recopilacion de chirvgia (Mexico, Antonio Ricardo, 1578) and Fray Agustín Farfán's Tractado breve de anothomia y chirvgia (Mexico, Antonio Ricardo, 1579) are other noteworthy Mexican scientific imprints of the sixteenth century.

In 1550 Pablos sent an agent, Juan López, to Spain to handle some business for him, and one item was to secure the services of a typefounder. On 24 September 1550 López made a contract on behalf of Pablos with Antonio de Espinosa,

Aue Maria gratia

plena dominus tecũ.

The first full-page wood engraving in an American book, in Pablos' edition of Gerson's Tripartito (1544).

Sumario cōpēdioſo delas quētas de plata y oro q̄ en los reynos del Piru ſon neceſſarias a los mercaderes: y todo genero de tratantes. Cō algunas reglas tocantes al Arithmetica.

Fecho por Juan Diez freyle.

Fray Juan Díez Freile's Sumario compendioso, printed by Pablos in 1556, the first mathematical book printed in America.

PHISICA, SPECV-
latio, Ædita per R.
P. F. ALPHONSVM A VERA CRVCE, AV-
gustinianæ familiæ Prouintialē, artiū, & sacræ Theologiæ Doctorem, atq;
cathedræ primæ in Academia Mexicana in noua Hispania moderatorē

¶ Accessit cōpendium sphœræ Cāpani ad complementū tractatus de cœlo.
¶ Excudebat Mexici Ioā. Pau. Brissē. Anno Dñicę incarnationis. 1557

Title-page of Fray Alonso de la Vera Cruz, Phisica speculatio, printed by Juan Pablos in 1557, from the John Carter Brown Library copy.

RECOGNITIO, SVM
mularum Reuerendi
PATRIS ILLDEPHONSI A VERA
CRVCE AVGVSTINIANI ARTIVM
ac ſacræ Theologiæ Doctoris apud indorum in-
clytam Mexicum primarij in Academia
Theologiæ moderatoris.

Title-page of Pablos' edition of Fray Alonso de la Vera Cruz' Recognitio svmmularum (1554), probably the first Roman type used in the New World.

"fundidor de letra", to come to Mexico and bring with him Diego de Montoya and to work as "fundidor y cortador" for Pablos for three years. Espinosa was not only a punchcutter but also a skilled bookmaker in general, and by 1554 the "gran cibdad de Tenochtitlan-Mexico" was beginning to acquire some fine printed books worthy of its sonorous name. Up through 1553 Pablos printed with four sizes of a monotonous rotunda, and his typography was wholly unimaginative. He apparently owned only two type ornaments, a Maltese cross and a unit of a vine pattern. He had some woodcut borders which he dissected and used in fantastic combinations. The bishop's hat with tassels that he used on the title page of the Doctrina breve of 1543 seems to have been a favorite.

Espinosa was a typographical reformer of first order. The three Pablos imprints of 1554, Fray Alonso de la Vera Cruz' Recognitio svmmularum, Fray Alonso's Dialectica resolutio (by Aristotle), and Francisco Cervantes de Salazar's Dialogos, contain the first Roman and italic types used in the New World, a tradition which was firmly established in short order. There are some unusually attractive wood engravings, in striking contrast to Pablos' pedestrian ornamentation. The Dialectica has a title page encompassed in an elaborate woodcut border, unmistakably Mexican in inspiration, but nevertheless essentially a copy of a border used a few years previously by Whitchurch in London. This remarkable case of typographical interrelationships between London and Mexico is one of the most striking of all early examples of the world-wide ramifications of the black art.

Chapter II

MEXICAN PRINTING IN THE SECOND HALF OF THE SIXTEENTH CENTURY

In 1559 Pablos' monopoly on printing in the Americas was broken. Espinosa returned to Spain and made a plea at the royal court for permission to set up a press in competition with Pablos', arguing that the prices charged by the latter were too high for individuals in moderate financial circumstances. A series of royal and viceregal cédulas printed by García Icazbalceta in his section on "Documentos" shows how the legalistic Spanish colonial administrators finally succumbed to Espinosa's urging in 1558 and 1559. During his active career as an independent printer (from 1559 until his death in 1576), Espinosa did some truly distinguished work. He used a large variety of types, much of which was undoubtedly cut and cast by himself (analyzed in detail by Emilio Valtón in his essay, "Algunas particularidades tipográficas de los impresores mexicanos del siglo XVI", in the festschrift, IV Centenario de la Imprenta en México, 1940). The most famous work printed by Espinosa was the magnificent Missale Romanum of 1561, a fine example of the service books printed in colonial Hispanic America, and some enthusiasts have even called it the handsomest book ever produced in America. Certainly it deserves a high rank with its imaginative use of red and black type, handsome wood engravings, and thoughtful typographical arrangement throughout. Incidentally, Espinosa was the only printer of his day to use a pressmark.

According to the late Henry R. Wagner's calculations in his essay on "Sixteenth Century Mexican Imprints" in the Wilberforce Eames festschrift (1924), 204 different Mexican titles from this period can now be located. In addition to Pablos and Espinosa, there were six other printers (including one woman) in sixteenth century Mexico who were responsible for this total. Upon Pablos' death (probably in 1560)

Missale romanum oꝛdinarium.

Missale Romanum
nuper adoptatum cõmodũ
quorũcũqꝫ sacerdotũ summa diligentia distin-
ctũ: atqꝫ ita ex nouo ordine digestũ vt appo
sitꝫ introitibꝰ, gradualibꝰ, offertorijs ꝛ cõ
munionibus oẽs misse sint in suis locꝫ
integre. In quo etiã adiuncte sunt
multe misse noue, ꝛ alia plurima
supaddita, q̃ in missalibꝰ hac-
tenꝰ ipsis desiderabãtur.
1561

This missal, printed by Antonio de Espinosa in 1561, is perhaps the most beautiful of the Mexican incunabula from the standpoint of typography.

¶ Arte dela lengua Mexi
cana y Caſtellana, compueſta por el muy Re
uerendo padre fray Alonſo de Mo
lina dela orden de Señor
ſant Franciſco.

¶ En Mexico en caſa de Pedro Ocharte. 1571

A philological publication by Pedro Ocharte just before his incarceration by the Holy Office. The engraving of the stigmata of St. Francis was frequently used in sixteenth century Mexican books.

DOCTRINA
CHRISTIANA, EN LENGVA ME
xicana muy neceſſaria: en la qual
ſe contienen todos los princi
pales myſterios de nue-
ſtra Sancta Fee ca-
tholica .:.

*COMPVESTA POR EL MVY REVE-
rendo Padre Fray Alonſo de Molina, de la orden
del glorioſo Padre Sant Franciſco.*

CON PRIVILEGIO.
En Mexico, En caſa de Pedro Ocharte.
M.D.LXXVIII.

Pedro Ocharte resumed work as an independent printer in 1578 with Fray Alonso de Molina's Doctrina christiana and Fray Juan de Córdoba's Arte en lengua Zapoteca.

his press passed to Pedro Ocharte (or possibly Ochart or Charte), born in Rouen about 1532. He probably arrived in Mexico about 1549. In 1561 or 1562 he married María de Figueroa, daughter of Juan Pablos, and the first imprint that bears his name is dated 1563. In 1570 he took a second wife, María de Sansoric, daughter of Pedro de Sansoric. This is a significant detail, since María de Sansoric, not María de Figueroa, as some bibliographers have argued, took over Ocharte's press when he ran afoul of the Holy Office in 1572. The imprint "Apud Viduam Petri Ocharte" on Father Alvarez' De institutione grammatica refers to María de Sansoric, not to the daughter of Juan Pablos. Ocharte's gallic esprit probably annoyed the intolerant minions of the Inquisition more than any overt heresy, and there is a hiatus of six years, from 1572 to 1578, when no major work came from his shop. Between 1572 and 1574, when Ocharte was actually incarcerated, his wife valiantly supervised the printing of "cartillas y los sumarios de Nuestra Señora del Rosario", and in 1576 he collaborated with Espinosa in producing a Graduale dominicale. Ocharte resumed independent printing in 1578 with the publication of an Arte en lengua zapoteca of Fray Juan de Córdoba and the Doctrina christiana, en lengua mexicana by Fray Alonso de Molina. His last publication was Agustín Farfán's Tractado brebe de medicina (1592; not to be confused with the Ricardo imprint of 1579, supra). Ocharte printed some thirty-five books, using an even richer variety of type (gothic, roman, italic, and music) than Espinosa and an unusually large number of woodcuts and elaborate initials. In addition to the type inherited from Pablos, Ocharte also patronized Espinosa's type foundry.

Pedro Balli, Mexico's fourth printer, came from Salamanca, although he was of French descent. He came to Mexico in 1569 as a bookseller, and he first appears as a printer in 1574 with Fray Juan Baptista de Lagunas' Arte y dictionario: con otras obras, en lengua Michuacana. His last imprint is Dionisio Ribera Flores' Relación historiada

ARTE Y DICTIO
NARIO: CON OTRAS
Obras, en lengua Michuacana. Cõpuesto por
el muy. R. P Fray Iuan Baptista de Lagu
nas, Prædicador, Guardian de sanct
Francisco, dela ciudad de Gua-
yangareo, y Diffinidor dela
Prouincia de Mechua-
can, y de Xalisco.
DIRIGIDAS AL MVY YLLV. Y. R.
señor Doctor dõ Antonio Morales ð Molina, Caua
llero dela ordẽ de Sãctiago, obispo meritissimo q̃ fue
de Mechuacã, y agora de Tlaxcala, del cõs. de su. M.

EN MEXICO,
En casa de Pedro Balli.
1574.

Title-page of the first recorded imprint of Pedro Balli, Mexico's fourth printer.

(1600). In his quarter of a century of activity as a printer, Balli produced more than sixty imprints, including books in indigenous languages and academic publications of the University of Mexico. One of the latter was the _Oratio in lavdem ivrisprudentiae_ (1596) by the printer's son, Juan Bautista Balli, an attorney of some distinction. Balli seems to have maintained close relations with his competitors, Espinosa and Ocharte, since he apparently exchanged type and wood engravings with them. It is also likely that he bought a good deal of equipment from the estates of Ocharte and Espinosa.

The fifth Mexican printer, of whom we will hear considerably more, was Antonio Ricardo, a Piedmontese who was born in Turin. A royal _cédula_ of 1569 refers to permission granted to Ricardo to go to Mexico, and he probably emigrated soon thereafter. It is not unlikely that he worked for Espinosa or Ocharte, probably the latter, since the names of Ocharte and Ricardo both appear on the imprint of Fray Juan de Córdoba's _Vocabvlario en lengva zapoteca_ (1578). The Jesuits arrived in Mexico in 1572, and during his short career as an independent printer in Mexico (1577 to 1579), Ricardo worked for them and even maintained his office in their Colegio de San Pedro y San Pablo. Ricardo's own work was quite notable from a typographical standpoint, for example, his edition of Fray Juan de la Anunciación's _Sermonario en lengua mexicana_ (1577).

The sixth printer in New Spain was the colorful Enrico Martínez, author of the _Desagüe_. His birthplace is variously located in Flanders, Andalusia, Hamburg, and Mexico itself. He printed from 1599 to 1611, although only one sixteenth century imprint may be assigned to his press, Fray Elias de San Juan Bautista's _Compendio de las excelencias, de la bvlla de la Sancta Cruzada, en lengua mexicana_ (1599). Martínez died in Cuauhtitlán on Christmas Eve 1632.

The seventh and last sixteenth century Mexican printer was Melchor (Melchior) Ocharte, probably the son of Pedro by his second marriage, born prior to 1574. His first imprint was a _Confessionario en lengua mexicana y castellana_

SERMONARIO

EN LENGVA

MEXICANA, DONDE SE CON-
TIENE(POR EL ORDEN DEL MISSAL
NVEVO ROMANO,) DOS SERMONES
en todas las Dominicas y Feſtiuidades principales de todo el año:
y otro en las Fieſtas de los Sanctos, con ſus vidas, y Comunes.

CON VN CATHECISMO EN LENGVA MEXICANA
y Eſpañola, con el Calendario. Compueſto por el reuerendo padre
Fray Iuan de la Annunciacion, Subprior del monaſte-
rio de ſant Auguſtin de Mexico.

DIRIGIDO AL MVY REVERENDO PADRE MAE-
ſtro fray Alonſo de la vera cruz, Prouincial de la orden de los
Hermitaños de ſant Auguſtin, en eſta nueua Eſpaña.

EN MEXICO, por Antonio Ricardo. M. D. L X X V I I.
Eſta taſſado en papel en pesos.

Title-page of one of Antonio Ricardo's first books printed in Mexico.

❋ CONFESSIONARIO ❋
EN LENGVA MEXI-
CANA Y CASTE
LLANA.

¶ Con muchas aduertencias muy necessarias
para los Confessores.

¶ Compuesto por el Padre Fray Ioan Baptista
de la orden del Seraphico Padre Sanct Francisco, lector de Theologia en esta prouincia del san
cto Euangelio, y guardian del conuento de San
tiago Tlatilulco.

❋ CON PRIVILEGIO. ❋
¶ En Sanctiago Tlatilulco, Por Melchior
Ocharte. Año de. 1599.

Title-page of the first imprint of Melchor (or Melchior) Ocharte, the seventh printer in Mexico.

(1599). He maintained his shop in the Franciscan college of Tlatelolco, and one of his employees was his half-brother Luis Ocharte de Figueroa, son of Pedro Ocharte and María de Figueroa.

It is of some interest to note that early Mexican printers were also booksellers. On the other hand, one Andrés Martín, who was not a printer, maintained a tienda de libros in 1541. Some social opprobrium seems to have been attached to the profession of bookselling, since in 1573 the Viceroy Enriquez referred to it as an oficio bajo.

Thanks to the labors of devoted scholars such as García Icazbalceta, Medina, Wagner, and others, we know a great deal about so-called Mexican "incunabula". It is a wonder, however, that enough early Mexican books have survived to give us as complete a picture as we have. The element — hurricanes, earthquakes, jungle humidity in the lowlands, and even volcanos — have conspired against the Mexican book. The polilla, a papyrophilic insect with a gargantuan appetite, is an unrelenting enemy of all books between Miami and Rio de Janeiro. A chronic scarcity of paper often discouraged book production throughout the colonial period. Then we must remember that most early Mexican books were printed with strictly practical objectives in mind, and a large proportion of surviving copies is grimy and dog-eared, often torn and lacking one or more pages. Some books have disappeared completely, a few without even so much as a clue that they ever existed. To others we have only allusions. Thus Fray Jerónimo de Mendieta refers to a Doctrina of Motolinia "que anda impresa". Fray Francisco Burgoa's Geografica descripcion (1674) states that Fray Domingo de Santa María had printed an Arte de lengua mixteca, of which we know nothing more. We have perhaps a score of such allusions to sixteenth-century Mexican books which may well have been printed but are now gone with the hurricane, the revolution, and the polilla.

Early Mexican printers produced utilitarian works needed

in the daily work of the church — catechisms, prayer books, liturgical works, and, above all, translations of religious works into the various languages of Mexico and vocabularies of these languages. Law, medicine, physical science, and belletristic letters were represented by only two or three works each. The clergy frowned on light reading, and there were no libros de caballerías, so beloved in Spain. Indeed, their importation was even forbidden. There was, however, a very substantial importation of scientific works from Europe, a trend that has not yet been changed after four and a half centuries. On the other hand, we know from a letter of a Viceroy, the Conde de La Coruña, dated 3 November 1582, that 9,000 dozen playing cards were produced in Mexico in that year and that they were considered superior to the Spanish product.

In a delightful essay entitled Some Reflections on the Book Arts in Early Mexico (Harvard College Library, 1945), Laurence C. Wroth describes the physical character of Mexican incunabula. The binding was usually in flexible vellum, ideal for a sheep-raising country. The European custom of covering oaken boards with leather took hold quite late in Mexico, for both boards and leather are comparatively expensive. Signatures were sewn on thongs of leather or vellum, and a minimum of glue was used. No attempt was made to round the back. Titles, if any, were simply written on the back or side in black ink. Sixteenth century Mexican binding was strong, practical, and durable, and to these primitive craftsmen we owe a heavy debt for having preserved many works that would have been destroyed in less substantial covers.

Chapter III

THE BEGINNING OF PRINTING IN PERU

Antonio Ricardo was not a failure in Mexico. During his active career as an independent printer in Mexico City, he produced ten books, or at least one every three months. Then he decided to move on to Peru, where in 1535 under Pizarro, Spanish soldiery had discovered and conquered riches that beggar the imagination. The new viceroyalty had thrived, and by 1551 it acquired the Universidad de San Marcos in Lima, oldest in the New World; but still there was no printing press. Ricardo may have been attracted either by the wealth of Peru or by the potential authors in the university, which was long to remain the intellectual capital of South America. A third possibility is that his patrons, the Jesuits, needed him in Lima. The first three Jesuits reached the viceroyalty of Peru in 1568, and others followed quickly on their heels. They may well have sent the word to the Colegio de San Pedro y San Pablo that a press in Lima (or La Ciudad de los Reyes, as it was first known and also appears in Ricardo's earliest imprints) would be of substantial help in realizing their aspirations to spiritual and temporal power.

Ricardo did not find it easy to move from Mexico to Peru. He was a foreigner, and as such he had to go to considerable trouble to get an entry permit for Peru. Ultimately, however, he was able to secure proper documentation and to book passage. He arrived in late 1580 or early 1581, but the first printed work from Lima that has survived is dated 1584. In any event, there is no evidence that Ricardo's services were not wanted, even though it might be difficult to get permission to set up a press. As early as 24 September 1572 the energetic Viceroy Francisco de Toledo wrote a letter (preserved in the Archivo de Indias) to the king urging that a catechism be translated into a composite Indian language, understood by all the people, and that it be printed either in Spain or in

New Spain. Ten years later, on 30 September 1583, the Real Audiencia of Lima wrote a letter to the king (also in the Archivo de Indias) restating the need for a catechism in Quechua and Aymará, pointing out that "a well-equipped printer from Mexico is in our city" and urging His Majesty to issue this printer a license at once. However, before the king could act, the Audiencia took matters into its own hands on 13 February 1584 and granted Ricardo an exclusive license to print certain books under the supervision of the Jesuits and to sell them at strictly regulated prices. Ricardo was in business, and his license to print was confirmed by a royal *cédula* issued from San Lorenzo del Escorial later in the year.

Ricardo's first and most urgent task was to get a catechism in print, for the Audiencia's communication of 30 September 1583 had stated unequivocally that "any delay affects adversely the character of these Indians, as they lack knowledge of the Christian Doctrine". The catechism was still not ready when the summer mail from the metropolis arrived. It contained, *inter alia*, a directive from the Crown concerning the decision of Gregory XIII to reform the calendar. Obviously, it was necessary to give widespread notification of this change, and Ricardo halted work on his catechism to print a *Pragmatica sobre los diez dias del año*, signed by the Audiencia on 14 July 1584. This is the first product of the printing press in South America, and the only surviving copies are in the John Carter Brown Library of Providence, Rhode Island, and the Harvard University Library.

Work on the catechism must have been nearly finished, for less than a month later, on 12 August 1584, the *auto* (certification) of the Audiencia was affixed to the *Doctrina christiana y catecismo para instrucción de los indios*. (The rather absurd rumor that a 1583 edition of this work was printed — without any official permission whatsoever! — dies hard. The copy in the Bartolomé Mitre Collection in Buenos Aires has a torn title page on which the title and the date 1583 are written in a crude hand, although the imprint date of M. D. LXXXVIIII, is clearly printed on the part of the page

DOCTRINA
CHRISTIANA,
Y CATECISMO PARA INSTRVCcion de los Indios, y de las de mas perſonas, que han de ſer enſeñadas en nueſtra ſancta Fé.
CON VN CONFESSIONARIO, Y OTRAS COSAS neceſſarias para los que doctrinan, que ſe contienen en la pagina ſiguiente.
COMPVESTO POR AVCTORIDAD DEL CONCILIO Prouincial, que ſe celebro en la Ciudad de los Reyes, el año de 1583.
Y por la miſma traduzida en las dos lenguas generales, de eſte Reyno, Quichua, y Aymara.

Impreſſo con licencia dela Real Audiencia, en la *Ciudad de los Reyes, por Antonio Ricardo primero Impreſſor en eſtos Reynos del Piru.*
AÑO DE M.D.LXXXIIII. AÑOS.
Eſta taſſado vn Real por cada pliego, en papel.

The second Lima imprint and the first major work published in Peru, the Doctrina christiana printed by Antonio Ricardo in 1584.

huápas payta, vi-
ac ſiruincanchic-
Amen Ieſus.

machita áropa
chañaſſataqui
cācana. Amen

Fin del Cateciſmo mayor.

This engraving, which appears at the end of the catechism in Ricardo's Doctrina christiana of 1584, was one of many that travelled vast distances in colonial America.

that is preserved. There is a facsimile of this title page in the *Gutenberg-Jahrbuch* for 1931, p. 216). This book of ninety-two leaves contains the Spanish text in a single column followed by the Quechua and Aymará texts in parallel columns. Besides being a monument of South American prototypography, this book also deserves recognition as a hammer-blow by the Jesuits against a moribund heathendom.

Ricardo printed two more books in 1585 for missionary purposes, a *Confesionario para los cvras de Indios* (possibly by Father Diego de Alcobaza, curate of Capi in Cuzco and son of an early *conquistador*) and a *Tercero cathecismo*, both in the same three languages as the *Doctrina christiana*. In 1586 came an *Arte, y vocabulario en la lengva general del Perv, llamada Quichua, y en la lengua Española*, attributed by Brunet and Medina to Father Domingo de Santo Tomás. We have no record of further activity by Ricardo until 1592, when he printed an *arancel real*. In 1594 Ricardo printed a fifteen-leaf pamphlet by Pedro Balaguer de Salcedo on the piracies of Sir Richard Hawkins, and the first vestige of a newspaper in the New World, a translation (on eight leaves) of a letter by "Ricardo Havqvines" to his father on his capture and the loss of his ship, the *Dainty*. Medina's monumental *La Imprenta en Lima, 1584-1824*, (4 vols., 1904-1907) records twelve sixteenth century imprints bearing Ricardo's name; and he describes twenty more in the next five years, ending with a *Sermón* by Fray Pedro Gutierrez Flores. In the next year *(1606)*, so we learn from the *Libro de funerales de la Parroquía del Sagracio*, the mortal remains of Antonio Ricardo of Turin, "primer impressor en estos Reynos del Peru", were laid to rest in the Iglesia de Santo Domingo in Lima.

In 1605 appeared the first Lima imprint by Francisco del Canto Lozano, Feliciano de Vega's *Relictio legis*, a pamphlet in Latin in fifteen leaves. Canto, son of a printer in Medina del Campo, came to Lima in 1586, but we first learn of him as a printer in 1604 when the viceroy, Don Luis de Velasco, granted him a license to print. Canto introduced the

TERCERO,

CATHECISMO

Y EXPOSICION DE LA

Doctrina Chriſtiana, por

Sermones.

PARA QVE LOS CVRAS Y OTROS

miniſtros prediquen y enſeñen a los Yndios

y a las demas perſonas.

CONFORME A LO QVE EN EL SANCTO

Concilio Prouincial de Lima ſe proueyo.

IMPRESSO CON LICENCIA DE LA

Real Audiencia, en la Ciudad de los Reyes, por Antonio Ricardo

primero Impreſſor en eſtos Reynos del Piru.

AÑO DE M.D.LXXXV.

Eſta taſſado vn Real por cada pliego, en papel.

Title-page of Ricardo's <u>Tercero cathecismo</u> (1585), in Quechua, Aymará and Spanish for the convenience of missionaries.

DOCTRINA
CHRISTIANA.

POr la señal de la sancta Cruz, de nuestros enemigos, libranos señor Dios nuestro.
En el nombre del Padre, y del Hijo, y del Spiritu Sancto. Amen.

QVICHVA.

SAncta cruzpa vnanchanraycu, aucaycu cunamanta, quispichihuaycu Dios apuycu.
Yayap, Churip, Spiritu Sanctop sutimpi. Amen Iesus.

AYMARA.

SAncta cruzana vnan chapalàycu. aucana cahàta nanaca quispijta, nanàcana Dios ápuha.
Anquina, Yocànsa, Spiritu sanctónsa sutipa na. Amen Iesus.

EL PATER NOSTER.

PAdre nuestro, que estas en los cielos, sanctificado sea el tu nombre. Venga a nos el tu reyno. Hagase tu voluntad, assi en la tierra, como en el cielo. El pan nuestro de cada dia, danos lo oy. Y perdona nos nuestras deudas, assi como nosotros

A las

Page from Ricardo's Doctrina christiana of 1584 showing the arrangement of Quechua, Aymará and Spanish texts.

refinement of two-color printing to Lima in 1608 with the Directorio espiritual of Father Arriaga, and he was also a bookseller and probably the author of an Arte, y vocabulario en la lengva general del Perv, llamada Quichua, y en la lengua Española issued by his press in 1614. Although Canto was a fairly prolific printer, by the standards of his country and his age, he was probably not a good business man. He was imprisoned briefly for debt in 1617, and the next year he issued his last book, Antonio Rodriguez de León Pinelo's Relacion de las fiestas qve a la Immaculada Concepcion de la Virgen N. Señora se hizieron en la Real Ciudad de Lima.

There is a first-class mystery associated with Canto's name. In 1612 four books by Father Ludovico Bertonio appeared with imprints such as the following: "Impressa en la Casa de la Compañia de Iesvs del pueblo de Iuli, que esta en la Provincia de Chucuyto, en la emprenta de Francisco del Canto, Año M.DC.XII.". The four titles include a great Vocabulario de la Lengua Aymará, a significant contribution to linguistics in some 900 pages, an Arte de la Lengua Aymará, a Vida de Christo, and a Confessionario in Aymará and Spanish. One thing only is certain: At some 12,000 feet above sea level a valiant band of Jesuits established a mission station and a college to facilitate the study of native languages at Julí on the Peruvian shore of Lake Titicaca. Between 1610 and 1612 a press, probably quite a different apparatus from the one producing books for Canto in Lima at the same time, was in operation in Juli. The Jesuits may have worked out some shadowy agreement with Canto whereby they could use his name, since he was a licensed printer, as a subterfuge to evade the vigilant zeal of the Audiencia in detecting unauthorized presses.

In 1613 the name of Pedro de Merchán Calderón appeared in the imprint of a book printed in Lima, but seven years passed before another book appeared over his name, and then only in three books printed in 1620. Merchán Calderón may have been associated with Canto during the seven years when we hear nothing of him.

In 1621 we have the first Lima imprint over the name of Jerónimo de Contreras, progenitor of one of the most famous of all Latin American printing families. He opened a printing shop in Seville in 1618 and began to print some works of the learned Franciscan friar Alonso de Herrera, who had just arrived from Lima. Evidently the latter persuaded Contreras to emigrate to Peru, and there he had a productive and fruitful career until 1639. A slight but significant early publication by Contreras was a four-page news-sheet captioned Nuevas de Castilla (1621). From then on such news-sheets containing resumés of the news brought by ship from Panama appeared fairly frequently, although the first American newspaper to be published periodically south of Mexico City was the Gazeta de Lima, beginning in January 1744. Native ability and a lucky marriage brought prosperity to Contreras, and in 1641 his son, José de Contreras, took over the business and managed it for forty-seven years. Next in the line of succession was a grandson of the founder, José de Contreras y Alvarado, Lima's only printer from 1686 to 1712. He secured the title of Royal Printer, and he was also printer to the Holy Office, the Tribunal of the Cruzada, and the Universidad de San Marcos. José's brother, Jerónimo de Contreras y Alvarado, who had been printing since 1677, took over in 1712; and the last book to bear the Contreras imprint appeared in 1720. Even after 1720, however, the daughters of the family maintained an interest in the press, and it was actually operated by persons associated with the Contreras family until 1779.

For the whole colonial period Medina records 3,948 titles (including a few duplications) for Peru and 12,412 for Mexico during the same period. Undoubtedly this proportion is characteristic of the relative importance and wealth of the two viceroyalties. Nevertheless, in Latin America as well as Saxon America we are constantly discovering colonial imprints, both at home and in such European depositories as the Public Record Office and the Archivo de Indias. There are discoveries to be made in the field of colonial American typography

Num. 14.

GAZETA

DE LIMA

QUE CONTIENE LAS NOTI-

cias de eſta Capital deſde 25. de Septiembre
haſta fin de Octubre de 1745.

LA ESCASEZ QUE SE EXPERIMENTA EN ESTA CA-
pital, de aquellas novedades, que todo bien conſiderado caben
en la Gazeta, es tanta à vezes, que no permite el formarla
con ſuficiente cuerpo; principalmente deſpues de los repetidos
avisos que nos han venido, tanto de adentro, como de fuera, de deſ-
cebar de ella algunos acaecimientos de poco, ó ningun importe para
las Provincias, aunque de algun valor, para los que viven en eſta Cor-
te, y que por eſto miſmo los ſaben mas á tiempo; y de abreviar otras
noti-

The Gazeta de Lima was the first American newspaper to be published regularly south of Mexico.

that may be as spectacular as anything that could be revealed about the mysteries of pre-Columbian history.

The content of Peruvian printing parallels that of Mexico and other Spanish colonies, with strong emphasis on religious texts (and particularly those destined for mission purposes), law, some history, some little science. Typographically the Lima imprints are less distinguished than are those of Mexico and Guatemala and even of some of the more remote South American communities. The typical Peruvian book was printed with poor ink of domestic manufacture, worn types, unimaginative vignettes and decorative pieces picked up second-hand in Spain and kept in use for a century or more, and on creaky presses that were refugees from the junk heap. Paper was scarce, but Medina points out that nevertheless editions ran into relatively high figures, from 500 to a thousand or more. Still many of the more important Peruvian authors sent their work to Spain or even to France and Germany to be printed. The colonial press of Latin America never was able to produce learned books in quantity, and Peru is a noteworthy example of this disproportion between the scholarly productivity of the friars and the lawyers and the current status of printing technology.

Chapter IV

PRINTING IN THE REDUCCIONES OF OLD PARAGUAY

When we speak of Paraguay in the sixteenth and seventeenth centuries, we must remember that this term originally was applied not only to the country between the Paraguay and Paraná Rivers but also to adjacent parts of Brazil, Uruguay and of the Argentine provinces of Buenos Aires, Entre Rios, Corrientes, Misiones, and part of Santa Fé. Indeed, the actual site of the beginning of printing in old Paraguay was in the present Argentine territory of Misiones. In 1620 Paraguay proper and Río de la Plata (or Buenos Aires) were made separate jurisdictions, but both were dependent on Lima until 1776 when the viceroyalty of Buenos Aires was created with Paraguay as one of its dependencies. Franciscans and, after them, Jesuits, had come to the Paraguay country in the decades after the founding of Asunción in 1535 by Juan de Ayolas, but it was only when a second band of Jesuits under Fathers José Cataldino, Simón Massetta, Marciel de Lorenzana and other leaders came to Paraguay in the first decade of the seventeenth century that the fantastic Jesuit _imperium in imperio_ of the _reducciones_ (settlements of converted Indians) became a reality. Until their expulsion in 1767 the Jesuits worked with the Guaraníes intensively, and the results are truly remarkable, not least of all for the history of printing in the southern half of South America.

Elsewhere in Spanish America Indians were regarded as _repartimientos_ or, later, _encomiendas_; but the Jesuit fathers erected a curious sort of communistic-theocratic state in old Paraguay in which they, as spiritual and temporal overlords, isolated their Indian wards from the corrupting influences of the Spanish colonial power. The Jesuit fathers taught the Indians trades and crafts, and the _reducciones_ were all but self-supporting. Indeed, when printing finally came to old Paraguay, only the paper had to be imported from the old world.

Printing was an early desideratum for the reducciones guaraníticas. In the minutes of the fifth Paraguayan provincial conference of Jesuits held in Córdoba in 1633 the following urgent wish was expressed: "Typographiam ad excudendam variorum Indicorum idiomatum, tum grammaticam, tum conciones pernecessarian enixe petit". In the same year an emissary of the Paraguayan fathers urged the Jesuit general, Mutio Vitelleschi, to send to Paraguay some brother from France, Flanders, or Germany who knew the art of printing. Despite repeated requests and even a directive from Vitelleschi to find a brother who could print, no practitioner of the black art is known to have entered the Río de la Plata at this time.

Nevertheless, the fathers were determined to have books, and so books they had. They taught the Guaraníes to copy European books with such meticulous care that Father Francisco Xarque or Jarque remarked in his Insignes misioneros (Pamplona, 1687) that it was difficult to differentiate between a missal printed in Antwerp and the same book after it had been copied by the Indian scribes. Several such books are described in detail by Father Guillermo Furlong, S. J., in his monumental Historia y bibliografía de las primeras imprentas rioplatenses, 1700-1850 (v. 1, 1953-). Even more interesting is the work which was done by the Guaraní xylographers. There is strong evidence on which to base a presumption that the Jesuits of old Paraguay had xylographic broadsides, pamphlets, or even books printed in the seventeenth century. A block found in Paraguay and presently owned by the Biblioteca Enrique Peña in Argentina is illustrated by a facsimile in Furlong's work. It is of the type that may have been cut by the Guaraníes, although it probably dates from a period subsequent to the expulsion of the Jesuits.

Actual letterpress printing did not come to the La Plata basin before the beginning of the eighteenth century; and the founders of the mission press were Father Juan Baptista Neumann of Vienna and Father José Serrano of Antequera in Andalucia. Neumann arrived at the Río de la Plata in 1690 at the age of thirty-two, and he died in Asunción in 1705 after winning honor for himself as an explorer and, above all, as a co-founder of the press in Paraguay. Serrano was born in 1634 and came to the Río de la Plata in 1658. He was head of the *reducciones* in the capacity of *superior* for a few months in 1695 and died in 1713 after a distinguished career as a teacher, scholar, and missionary.

The beginning of printing in old Paraguay is recorded by Father Antonio Sepp in his *Continuatio laborum apostolicorum . . . in Paraquaria* (Ingolstadt, 1710) with a prologue dated 8 December 1701: "Hoc ipso anno (1700) J. Joannes Bapt. Neumann, ex Provincia Bohemiae, *Martyrologium Romanum*, quohuiusque plurimae Reductiones carebant, typis impressum, luci publicae exposuit, et licet impressioni Europae inaequales sunt litterae, sunt tamen legibles". No copy of this first book, most likely printed in Loreto, in old Paraguay, has survived, nor has a copy of the 1709 edition (probably issued to correct many errors in the first), the fourth book printed in Paraguay; but we know of their existence from subsequent inventories of Jesuit libraries. We cannot be absolutely sure that the two *Martirologios* were in Guaraní, but it is likely that they were, or at least that they were bilingual.

Another basic document is a letter of 6 January 1696 from Tirso González, the Jesuit General in Rome, to Lauro Núñez, the *provincial* of Paraguay. González refers to translations into Guaraní of Pedro de Rivadeneira's *Flos Sanctorum*, and of Juan Eusebio Nieremberg's *Diferencia entre lo temporal y eterno*, being undertaken by Father Serrano; and, even more significant, he expresses the desire that a press be set up so that these books may be made accessible to literate Indians. Serrano completed the translation of the *Flos sanctorum* in 1699, and on 18 September 1700 both this volume and the translation of the *Diferencia* received the approval of the dean of the Cathedral of Asunción. No copy of the printed edition of the *Flos sanctorum* has survived, but we have a record of its existence in Jesuit inventories compiled before the expulsion. Fortunately, we have two complete

DELA DIFERENCIA ENTRELO
TEMPORAL YETERNO
CRISOL DE DESENGAÑOS, CONLA ME
MORIA DELAETERNIDAD POSTRIMERIAS HV
MANAS, YPRINCIPALES MISTERIOS DIVINOS
POR EL
P. IVAN EVSEBIO NIEREMBERG
DELA COMPAÑIA DE
IESVS
Y TRADVCIDOEN LENGVA GVARANI
POR EL PADRE
IOSEPH SERRANO
DELA MISMA COMPAÑIA
DEDICADO ALAMAGESTAD DEL
ESPIRITVSANTO
CONLICENCIADELEXELENTISSIMO
SEÑOR
D.MELCHORLASSODELAVE
GA PORTO CARRERO
Virrey, Governador, y Capitan general del Peru
Impresso en las Doctrinas Año de M.D.CC.V.

Title-page of De la diferencia entre lo temporal y eterno, first surviving Paraguayan imprint.

copies of the *Diferencia*. It bears an unequivocal imprint, "Impresa en las Doctrinas Año de M.D.CC.V.". The actual place was most probably Loreto. The book contains 438 double-columned pages in small folio, abundantly illustrated with woodcuts and decorative initials.

All the valid evidence points to Father Neumann as the creator of the press and types used in Paraguay. *The Martirologio* was probably a rather crude production, since it had to be revised in 1709; but Father Serrano seems to have joined with the Austrian to perfect the press and the types in order to produce the creditable *Diferencia*. Certainly both of them were in Loreto not later than the end of 1701, and it is unthinkable that the two should not have cooperated in developing the new press in both technical and editorial matters. Contrary to various speculations that the types used at Loreto were cast from pure lead, brass, or bronze, Furlong cites evidence that suggests strongly that the type metal was a more or less conventional alloy of lead and tin. In any event it seems most likely that the type was cast in Paraguay. Another unfounded allegation holds that the *Diferencia* and possibly other early Paraguay imprints were produced clandestinely, despite the specific note on the title-page of the *Diferencia* that it was produced "con licencia del exelentissimo Señor D. Melcho Lassa de la Vega Porto Carrera Virrey . . . del Peru". The Jesuits did not have to print clandestinely, and, in fact, the viceroy's written permission, dated 5 September 1703, exists today in Rio de Janeiro and is cited in full by Furlong.

The most fascinating possible relic of the press of old Paraguay is a fragment of what Medina and others allege to be the remains of the first press in Loreto. The fragment so revered by Medina (probably at the firm and patriotic insistence of General Mitre) is now in the Museo del Cabildo in Buenos Aires, where it has been fully reconstructed. The press does undoubtedly date from a period prior to the nineteenth century, but neither Medina, Mitre, nor any of the historians who accepted their notions about the old fragment have been able to cite any real evidence that this press was

INSTRVCCION
PRACTICA
PARA
Ordenar Santamente la vida; que
ofrece El P. Antonio Garriga de
la Compania de Ieſus.
Como brebe memorial, y recuerdo
à los que hazen los exercicios eſpi-
rituales de S. Ignacio de lo
yola Fundador de la
miſma Com-
pania.

En Loreto, con licencia de los
Superiores en la Imprenta de
la Compañia

Año de 1713

Paraguayan book of 1713 showing imprint of Loreto.

used by the early printers of Paraguay. The final and essential material for printing, paper, was imported from Spain. It was the only thing that the Jesuits did not produce, and, indeed, they never succeeded in bringing a paper industry to the Río de la Plata country.

Excluding spurious and doubtful titles, Furlong describes twenty-three Paraguay imprints issued during the period from 1700-1727. Nine titles survive, and of the other fourteen, nine are known only from Sepp's Geschichte von Paraguai (1712; Munich, Staatsarchiv, Hs. 275). We may grieve over all the lost titles, but one in particular, Father Segismundo Aperger's Tratado breve de medicina (1720), is a special tragedy, for it was the first scientific treatise printed south of Peru.

The imprints on the surviving titles indicate that printing was done in Loreto, Santa María la Mayor, San Javier, and possibly a fourth locality, which Furlong suggests might be Candelaria, the see of the superior of the Jesuit missions in old Paraguay. All four places are located in the present Argentine federal territory of Misiones. There has been considerable debate as to whether there were several presses or one press moved from place to place. Various bibliographers have supported both views, and no real conclusion has been reached.

After 1727 we hear no more of the press of the Jesuit missions, and not until thirty-eight years later was there any printing anywhere in the La Plata basin, or at least none that is known at present. Various theories have been advanced to explain this abrupt end of one of the most fantastic printing ventures in history. There is evidence that the crown was not completely satisfied that printing by the Jesuits in the New World was a good thing. A likely explanation of the cessation of printing in Paraguay is that the uncomprehending Spanish colonial civil administrators disapproved of the use of indigenous dialects and tried to stamp them out. It was feared that continuing use of the native idiom was one of the strongest of all ties to freedom and independence, and we have substantial evidence of efforts to hispanicize the aborigines. There is

MANUALE

Ad vſum

Patrum Societatis

IESV.

Qui in Reductionibus

PARAQVARIÆ

verſantur

Ex *Rituali Romano*

ac Toletano

decerptum

Anno Domini MDCCXXI

Superiorum permiſsu

Laureti typis P.P. Societatis IESV.

Paraguayan book of 1721 showing imprint of Loreto.

ARTE
DE LA LENGUA GUARANI
POR EL P. ANTONIO RUIZ
DE
Montoya
DE LA COMPAÑIA
DE
JESUS
Con los Eſcolios Anotaciones
y Apendices
DEL P. PAULO RESTIVO
de la miſma Compañia
Sacados de los papeles
DEL P. SIMON BANDINI
y de otros.
En el Pueblo de S. MARIA La Mayor
El AÑO de el Señor MDCCXXIV

Paraguayan book of 1724 showing imprint of Santa María La Mayor.

abundant evidence that no love was lost between viceregal authorities and the Jesuits, and the former placed many obstacles in the way of the latter. It is one of the curious facts of history that Anglo-Saxon Americans had no official obstacles placed in their way when they attempted to teach the Indians and publish in their language, but today Indian dialects in the United States have no importance as a linguistic element. Precisely the opposite is true in much of Spanish America and Luso-America.

EXPLICACION
DE EL
CATECHISMO
EN LENGUA GUARANI
PORNICOLAS YAPUGUAI
CON DIRECCION
DEL P. PAULORESTIVO
DELA COMPAÑIA
DE
JESUS

En el Pueblo de S. MARIA La Mayor.
AÑO DE MDCCXXIV

Paraguayan book of 1724 showing imprint of Santa Maria La Mayor.

Chapter V

THE BEGINNING OF PRINTING IN THE RÍO DE LA PLATA REGION

Today the great city of Buenos Aires and its hinterland are more important economically than any other region of Latin America, and it is somewhat astonishing to realize that printing did not come to the rich lands at the mouth of the Río de la Plata until the latter part of the eighteenth century. The fact is simply that the population of Buenos Aires was relatively small (in 1770 there were slightly more than 20,000, of whom half were Negroes or civil and military officials), and for various reasons we cannot list in detail here, the cultural interests of the capital of the southernmost viceroyalty were relatively slight. Remote Chuquisaca (Sucre) or Guamanga (Ayacucho) had a more substantial cultural life than colonial Buenos Aires.

Thus it was not in Buenos Aires but in Córdoba de Tucumán where the first printing was done in Argentina. In that interior city, some 700 kilometers from Buenos Aires, the seventh university of colonial Spanish America, the Jesuit Colegio Máximo de Córdoba, became the Universidad de San Ignacio in 1622 by papal and royal authority. The Jesuits, always indefatigable in their "peculiar care in the education of boys", found a home for their new university in the Convictorio de Montserrat and developed it into an important seat of learning.

It was not until 1750, however, at the twenty-fourth Congregación Provincial, that the need for a press was expressed. Father Pedro de Arroyo and Father Carlos Gervasoni were elected to represent that Congregation at the courts of Rome and Madrid and to procure the necessary printing equipment. Unfortunately the star of the Jesuits was setting. Arroyo died in Madrid in 1753, and Gervasoni was expelled from Spain because of the vigor with which he defended the interests of the Indians in the matter of the Treaty of Limits.

CLARISSIMI VIRI

D.D. IGNATII

DUARTII ET

QUIROSII,

COLLEGII MONSSERRATENSIS CORDUBÆ IN AMERICA CONDITORIS,

LAUDATIONES QUINQUE,

QUAS

EIDEM COLLEGIO REGIO

BARNABAS ECHANIQUIUS O.D.

Cordubæ Tucumanorum Anno. MDCCLXVI,
Typis Collegii R. Monſſerratenſis.

Title-page of Laudationes (1766) in honor of Dr. Ignacio Duarte y Quirós, the first surviving imprint of Córdoba de Tucumán.

(✝) 1

CLARISSIMI VIRI

D. D. IGNATII DUARTII ET QUIROSII

LAUDATIO I.

NESSE MAJORUM NOBILITATI vim ſuam, quæ non ſinat degenerare minores ab avita gloria, is neget unus, qui & ignobilis ipſe ſit, nulliſque majoribus, nec magni illud vatis audierit unquam:

> Fortes creantur fortibus, & bonis.
> Nec imbellem feroces
> Progenerant aquilæ columbam. (1)

Certè heroicis illis temporibus ſola commendatio virtutis diſtinxit è plebe nobiles. Nam ſiquis arte quadam dicendi & eloquentià diſperſos homines, & vagantes more belluarum in unum locum conjunxerat; ſiquis ingenio, & pru-

B den-

(1) *Horat. Lib.* 4. *Od.* 4.

First page of text of the <u>Laudationes</u> (Córdoba, 1766).

Nevertheless, Gervasoni was able to buy a press, types, and other equipment in Italy and ship the whole to Córdoba in 1758 or soon thereafter.

A German Jesuit, Pablo Karrer, a printer by profession, had been secured to operate the press, but he did not reach the Río de la Plata until 1764. Furlong records six publications from this press in 1766 and 1767, the year of the expulsion of the Jesuits from all the Spanish dominions and the confiscation of their property. The first and perhaps most important Córdoban imprint was a collection of five panegyrics on the university's greatest benefactor, Dr. Ignacio Duarte y Quirós, by Father José Peramás. A facsimile was produced in 1937 by the Instituto de Estudios Americanistas of the University of Córdoba. The other works are religious manuals and publications relating to the University. The end came quickly in 1767. The Franciscans occupied the Convictorio. On the orders of the Viceroy Juan José de Vértiz y Salcedo the press and the equipment were sent to Buenos Aires in 1780.

Thus ended the first Argentine press of which we have a clear and unequivocal history. José Torre Revello produced evidence in the Boletín of the Instituto de Investigaciones Históricas, Buenos Aires, in 1943 that there may have been one or more small presses in Buenos Aires prior to the removal of the Jesuit press from Córdoba, but there is no evidence whatsoever to identify the printer or the shop. Until we can learn more about these presses, we cannot date the beginning of printing in Buenos Aires prior to 1780.

Three men, Viceroy Vértiz, a Portuguese bookseller named José Silva y Aguiar, and Manuel Ignacio Fernández, governor of the city, were largely responsible for the introduction of printing to Buenos Aires. As early as 1778 Vértiz wrote to the Franciscans in Córdoba inquiring about the press, now idle for nearly a dozen years. In 1779 Fernández had addressed a letter to the royal minister, José Gálvez, requesting a press for the community, largely for official purposes. He even attached a list of necessary types

REGLAS,

Y CONSTITVCIONES, QVE HAN DE GVARDAR los Colegiales del Colegio Real de N. S. de Monſerrate.

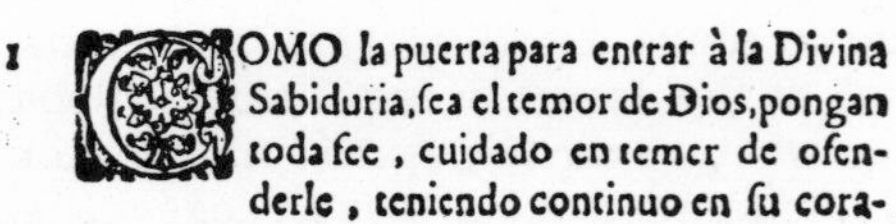

1 COMO la puerta para entrar à la Divina Sabiduria, ſea el temor de Dios, pongan toda fee, cuidado en temer de ofenderle, teniendo continuo en ſu coraçon ſu Santa Ley.

2 El blanco de ſus eſtudios ſea el ſervir, y complacer à la Mageſtad de Dios, ratificando à menudo eſta intencion, y pidiendo los govierne, y enderece para tan alto fin; y aſsi al entrar en el Colegio Confeſſaràn, y Comulga-

First page of text of Reglas y constitvciones qve han de guardar los Colegiales del Colegio Real de N.S. de Monserrate (Córdoba, 1766-1767).

and a statement on the "modo de hacer tinta" (taken from contemporary texts) to his petition. It is probable that Silva y Aguiar was the source of these rather detailed specifications. Gálvez approved Fernández' request, but before Madrid could act, the energetic Vértiz had followed up his letter of 1778 to Córdoba, and early in 1780 the old Jesuit press with its equipment was in Buenos Aires.

Vértiz' regime as viceroy (1778-1784) was one of the most progressive and enlightened in the colonial history of Spanish America. Among his other contributions to the social betterment of Buenos Aires was the establishment of the Casa de Niños Expósitos (foundling home) in 1779. Vértiz had the happy idea of putting the press under the jurisdiction of the Niños Expósitos as a source of income for that institution. Soon after the press arrived Silva y Aguiar offered to supervise its operation for the Niños Expósitos, and Vértiz accepted his offer. The press was immediately put to work even without the customary royal approval. The viceroy and his advisors must have felt that they were on reasonably safe grounds, and the crown actually gave formal approval in 1782 — after some 150 separate items had come off the press.

Silva y Aguiar's enthusiasm was not matched by technical skill as a printer, and, moreover, he would hardly have wanted to give up his bookselling business for printing. He ascertained that a dragoon corporal stationed across the river in Montevideo, one Agustín Garrigós of Alicante, was a trained printer; and, through Vértiz, Silva arranged for Garrigós' detachment and reassignment in Buenos Aires. (The absurdly romantic legend that Garrigós accepted the job only on the condition that he be allowed to choose an orphan girl as a bride was effectively punctured in 1929 by F. de Ugarteche in his La imprenta argentina; sus orígenes y desarrollo). Garrigós was on the job in August 1780 and he soon had several helpers, at least three of whom were also soldiers.

The press of the Niños Expósitos was a busy office from the beginning. Furlong records fifteen separate imprints for 1780, sixty-one for 1781, and ninety-five for 1782. The vast majority were official documents in the form of broadsides, and, indeed these were the exclusive products of the press in 1780. As the first Buenos Aires imprint, Furlong and other bibliographers list a rather tastefully printed little broadside captioned "Letrilla, que llevaba por registro en su Breviario la Seráfica Madre Santa Teresa de Jesús". The first work recorded for 1781 is an almanac, of which no copy is now known, although Antonio Zinny described it in a fragmentary fashion in his Bibliografía histórica de las Provincias Unidas del Río de la Plata, 1780-1821 (1875). Other products of the press in 1781 were a rather extensive pastoral letter of the bishop of Córdoba de Tucumán, a catechism, a couple of news-sheets, several novenas, and other religious works.

In spite of Silva y Aguiar's distinguished services in behalf of printing in Buenos Aires, his efforts did not meet with full favor in the eyes of the authorities. He was the object of rather grave accusations of mismanagement; and in the fall of 1783 Captain Alfonso Sánchez Sotoca, who had made an extensive report on Silva's administration of the press, replaced the Portuguese bookseller as the director. The military man ran the press effectively for six years, during all of which Silva made every effort to regain control. The latter finally succeeded in July 1789 and continued for five years. The press subsequently had various other administrators, including Garrigós (1799-1804); and in 1825 the "Imprenta de los Expósitos" finally became the "Imprenta del Estado", although the old press had probably been replaced five years earlier.

While this essay is primarily designed to cover printing in the colonial period, it would be improper not to mention the first printing in a cultural center as important as Montevideo is today, especially in view of the rather spectacular auspices under which the art arrived in the Banda Oriental. Montevideo had no press in the eighteenth century, and as late as 1807 it was only an overgrown provincial capital of 4,300 souls. However, the rather sordid story of the English efforts to invade the regions of the Río de la Plata in

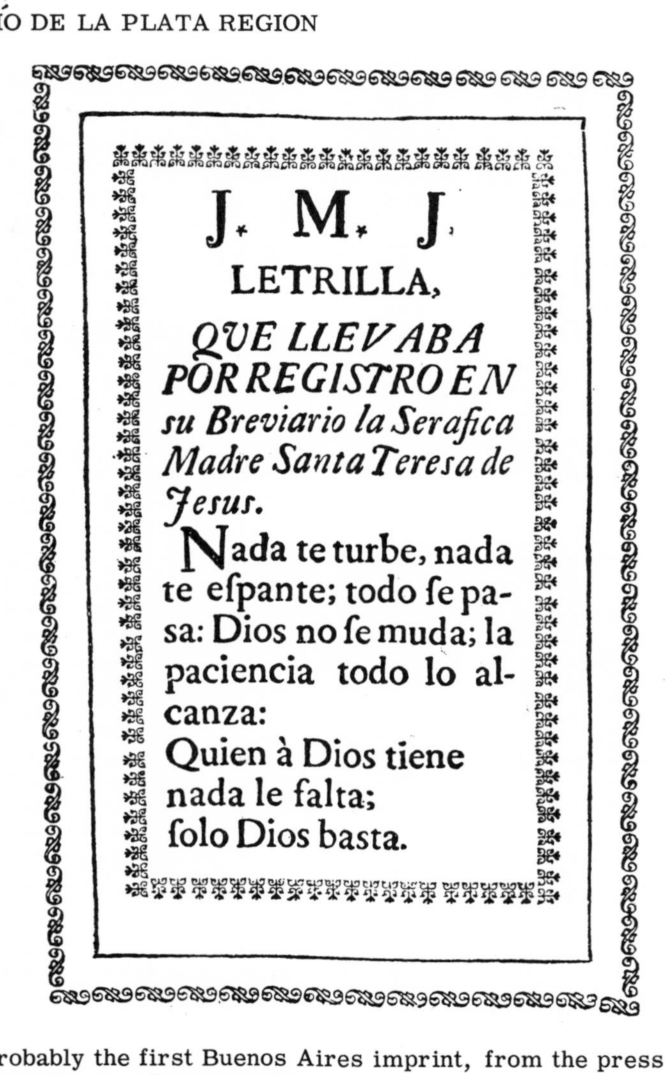

J. M. J.

LETRILLA,

QVE LLEVABA POR REGISTRO EN su Breviario la Serafica Madre Santa Teresa de Jesus.

Nada te turbe, nada te eſpante; todo ſe pasa: Dios no ſe muda; la paciencia todo lo alcanza:
Quien à Dios tiene
nada le falta;
ſolo Dios basta.

Probably the first Buenos Aires imprint, from the press of the Niños Expósitos in 1780.

(1)

EXTRACTO DE LAS

Noticias recibidas de Europa por la via de Portugal.

GAZETA DE LISBOA

1. DE MAYO 1781.

Madrid 24. de Abril.

Abemos por las Cartas de los Comandantes Generales de Mar, y Tierra del bloqueo de *Gibraltar* con fecha de 12. del corriente, que en el mismo dia llegó à aquella Plaza el Comboy *Ingles*, compuesto de 28. Navios de Linea, 9. de los quales eran de 3. puentes, 10. Fragatas, y 97. Embarcaciones de Transporte. Habiendo dado los Generales anticipadamente sus órdenes para hacer lo que fuese mas idóneo para daño de los Enemigos, el de Mar luego que las Embarcaciones empezaron à embocar el *Estrecho*, embiò al Mayor General *D. Ventura Moreno* con 1[illegible]. Lanchas armadas con artillería, y 4. con bombas mandidas por Oficiales à *Punta Carnero*, las que fondeandose en linea, salieron al encuentro con tal intrepidez, resolucion, y método, que haciendo fuego contra una Fragata, y dos Navios, que venian por cabeza del Comboy, los obligaron à responder con toda su artilleria, durando este ataque 2. horas, hasta que las dichas Lanchas se retiraron por haber refrescado el viento,

One of the news-sheets printed in Buenos Aires in 1781.

1806 and 1807 had a salubrious effect on Uruguay in at least one respect. General Samuel Auchmuty must have thought he came to found a new empire, for the well equipped invasion fleet even included a printing press (much as Napoleon's forces introduced printing to Egypt with a shipboard press at Alexandria and Cairo in 1798). Soon after Auchmuty assumed control of Montevideo in February 1807, a weekly, The Southern Star — La Estrella del Sur, began to appear; but it lasted only until 11 July 1807, after General John Whitlocke's ignominious defeat and the withdrawal of English forces from the Río de la Plata. A facsimile was issued in 1942 by the Instituto Histórico y Geográfico del Uruguay under the editorship of Ariosto D. González. We know next to nothing about the printers of The Southern Star, but Furlong has provided an admirable summary of the various conjectures.

The English press in Montevideo had little or no influence, but three years later La Gazeta de Montevideo was founded to support the royalist cause. The press was sent by the Infanta Carlota Joaquina from Rio de Janeiro in 1810, and it is the true cornerstone of printing in the Banda Oriental. For this reason the Imprenta de la Ciudad de Montevideo was also popularly known as the Imprenta de Carlota. At least this one positive result may be traced to the unhappy rivalry between Argentina and Brazil for Uruguay in the two decades following the English invasion.

Chapter VI

PRINTING IN MEXICO AND CENTRAL AMERICA IN THE SEVENTEENTH AND EIGHTEENTH CENTURIES

The third place in which printing was established in Latin America, and, indeed, the fourth in the Americas (after Mexico, Lima, and Cambridge) was the handsome old city of Puebla de los Ángeles. So-called from the pretty tradition that two angels added as much to the walls of the magnificent Doric Cathedral (1552-1649) as the workmen completed on the preceding day, Puebla was founded in 1532, became an episcopal see in 1550), and has always been recognized as the second city of Mexico in cultural importance. The origins of printing in Puebla are as obscure and controversial as they are in Mexico City, and Medina has explored the problem fully in his *La imprenta en la Puebla de los Ángeles (1640-1821)* (1908).

The legend that a book was printed in Puebla in 1634 dies hard, and it still appears in cheap guide books by chauvinistic *angelopolitanos*. The first Puebla imprint of which we have positive knowledge is Father Mateo Salcedo's *Arco triunfal: emblemas, geroglificos y poesias con que la ciudad de la Puebla recibio al Virrey de Nueva España, Marques de Villena* with the simple imprint, "Impreso en la Puebla de los Ángeles, 1640". We know of no printing in Puebla in 1641 or 1642, but five titles appeared in 1643, *viz*., three rather slight religious tracts without designation of printer, and the humanitarian Bishop Juan de Palafox y Mendoza's *Historia real sagrada* (En la Ciudad de los Ángeles, por Francisco Robledo, Impressor del Secreto del Santo Oficio, Año de 1643), and Bartolome Venavides y de la Cerda's *Sermon* (En la Puebla de los Ángeles, por Diego Gutiérrez, Año de 1643).

Robledo's name is the first to appear on a Puebla imprint, but was he responsible for the *Arco triunfal*? He started printing in Mexico City in 1640 and continued until 1647, when he probably died. He came into contact with the bibliophilic

Bishop Palafox in 1642, and in the same year he became printer in secret to the Holy Office. It seems likely that Palafox persuaded Robledo to send part of his equipment to Puebla to print the Historia real sagrada and probably also a Carta pastoral (one of the three 1643 Puebla imprints without a printer's name). Robledo was settled in Mexico before books appeared over his imprint in Puebla, and it is unlikely that he printed the Arco triunfal, unless (and this is improbable) he lived for a short while in Puebla before going to Mexico in 1640.

Medina suggests another possibility for the honor of being Puebla's first printer. The enigmatic Juan Blanco de Alcázar printed some of the most typographically distinguished works of the seventeenth century in Mexico between 1617 and 1627 (notably Fray Antonio del Pozo's Monastica theologica, 1618). He disappeared completely for almost two decades, and suddenly, in 1646, his name reappears on a Puebla imprint. He was the printer of four rather slight works between 1646 and 1650. Blanco de Alcázar cannot be completely eliminated as Puebla's first printer. Medina finds no reason to attribute the Arco triunfal to Diego Gutiérrez, whom we know to have been active as a printer in Mexico City from 1628 to 1634. Gutiérrez again appears in Mexico City in 1643 but he moved in that year to Puebla, printed the Venavides Sermon, and disappeared from typographical history.

The most important of all Puebla printers was Diego Fernández de León, who practiced his craft in the City of the Angels from 1683 to 1709. His establishment was a pretentious one, and in 1690 he had at least five assistants. In 1688 he received a large shipment of Dutch type from Spain, and from then on he called his shop the "Plantiniana". He was the first Puebla printer to use a device (a lion with a banner emblazoned with the initials DFDL), and his work was typographically attractive and textually significant. It is of some interest to note that the great printing firm of Calderón, which dominated publishing in Mexico City in the whole latter half of the seventeenth century, also boasted of its Dutch type by applying to itself the designations of "Plantin Press" and "Antwerp Press".

HISTORIA

REAL

SAGRADA,

LVZ

DE PRINCIPES.

Y

SVBDITOS.

Dedicada

AL PRINCIPE NVESTRO SEÑOR.

POR

EL ILLVSTRISSIMO, Y REVERENDISSIMO,
Don Iuan de Palafox, y Mendoça, Obiſpo de la Puebla de los Angeles, del Conſejo de ſu Mageſtad.

CON LICENCIA,

En la Ciudad de los Angeles, *Por Franciſco Robledo*, Impreſſor del Secreto del Santo Oficio.
Año de 1643.

Title-page of the fourth surviving imprint from Puebla de los Angeles, the noted Bishop Juan de Palafox y Mendoza's Historia real sagrada (1643).

HISTORIA DE LA SINGVLAR VIDA, DE EL VE=NERABLE HERMANO FRAY CHRISTO-val de Molina Religioſo Lego de la Orden de N. P. San Auguſtin.

Hijo de el illuſtriſſimo Convento de Nueſtra Señora de Gra=cia de la miſma Orden; de la Ciudad de la Puebla de los Angeles donde reciviò el habito, y muriò.

ESCRITA POR EL PADRE LECTOR Fr. NICOLAS Ponze de Leon, Religioſo de la miſma Orden. Año de 1686.

DEDICADA AL CAPITAN DIEGO DE AN-drada Peralta, Alcalde Ordinario, que fuè en la muy Noble Ciudad de la Puebla de los Angeles; y Sobrino de el Vene-rable Hermano.

CON LICENCIA

En la Puebla de los Angeles por Diego Fernandez de Leon. Año de 1686.
Vendenſe en ſu Tienda en la eſquina de la Plaça en la Calle de Cholula.

Title-page of life of Cristóbal de Molina, printed in 1686 by Diego Fernández de León, the most important of the Puebla printers of the seventeenth century.

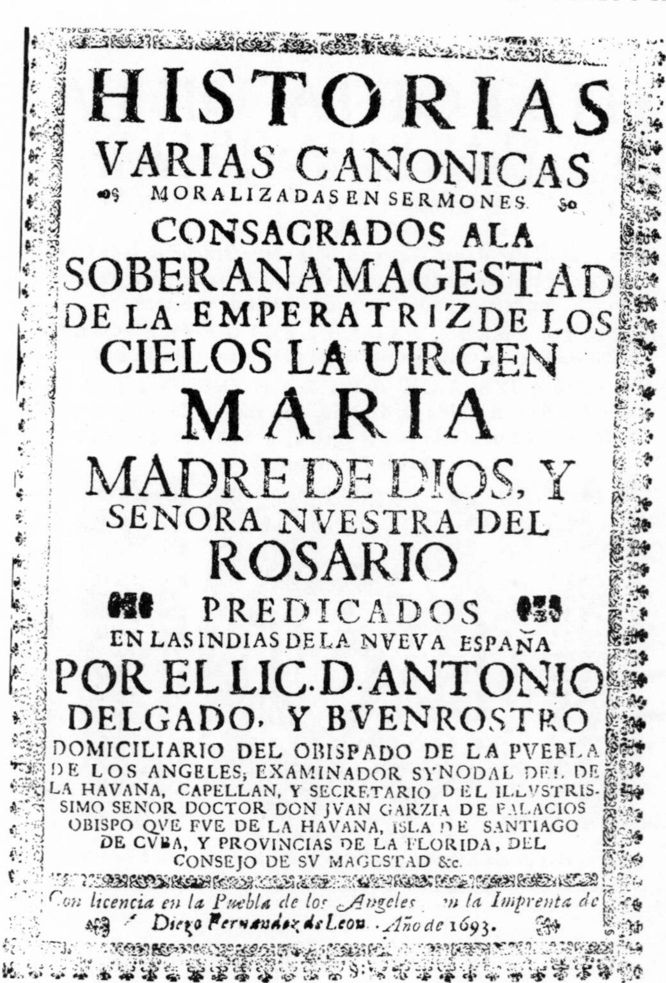
HISTORIAS
VARIAS CANONICAS
MORALIZADAS EN SERMONES.
CONSAGRADOS ALA
SOBERANA MAGESTAD
DE LA EMPERATRIZ DE LOS
CIELOS LA UIRGEN
MARIA
MADRE DE DIOS, Y
SENORA NVESTRA DEL
ROSARIO
PREDICADOS
EN LAS INDIAS DE LA NVEVA ESPAÑA
POR EL LIC. D. ANTONIO
DELGADO, Y BVENROSTRO
DOMICILIARIO DEL OBISPADO DE LA PVEBLA
DE LOS ANGELES, EXAMINADOR SYNODAL DEL DE
LA HAVANA, CAPELLAN, Y SECRETARIO DEL ILVSTRIS-
SIMO SENOR DOCTOR DON JVAN GARZIA DE PALACIOS
OBISPO QVE FVE DE LA HAVANA, ISLA DE SANTIAGO
DE CVBA, Y PROVINCIAS DE LA FLORIDA, DEL
CONSEJO DE SV MAGESTAD &c.

Con licencia en la Puebla de los Angeles en la Imprenta de Diego Fernandez de Leon. Año de 1693.

Title-page of Antonio Delgado y Buenrostro's *Historias varias canónicas* (Puebla, Diego Fernández de León, 1693).

By the eighteenth century printing was an established industry in Mexico City and Puebla, and the growing wealth of colonial society provided an outlet for an ever greater variety of books. Books on mining, current events, history, geography, and biography appear. Strangely enough, printing did not come to Guadalajara, Puebla's rival for the rank of Mexico's second city, until 1793. In the next year Veracruz acquired a press. A press was installed in Oaxaca in 1811, although almost one full century earlier there had been another press in the southern metropolis. In 1720 the Doña Francisca Flores issued Fray Sebastian de Santander's Sermon funebre on Mother Iacinta Maria Anna of the Convent of St. Catherine of Siena, a pamphlet of twelve leaves. There is no other extant piece of printing from this press, and we know nothing of what may have happened to the equipment. Doña Francisca died in 1725, and we know only that she made the Convent of St. Catherine her sole beneficiary. When Oaxaca again acquired a printing house, it was under the direction of a priest named José María Idiaquez. In the midst of the revolutionary disturbances of the day Idiaquez was compelled to found type, a feat that rivals the work of Antonio de Espinosa and of the Jesuits of old Paraguay.

The third early center of printing in Spanish North America and the fifth in the western hemisphere was Guatemala, and again here there has been some uncertainty concerning the first Guatemalan imprint. (It must be remembered that prior to 1779 Guatemala in an imprint refers to what we now know as Antigua, or Santiago de los Cabelleros la Nueva, the beautiful old city destroyed by the earthquake of 1773). Medina, in his classic La Imprenta en Guatemala (1660-1821) (1910), demolishes effectively the tradition that there was printing in Guatemala before 1660. It was the distinguished Father Payo Enriquez de Ribera who was responsible for bringing the black art to the land of the Quetzal. The son of the Duke of Alcalá and an Augustinian since the age of sixteen (in 1628), Fray Payo was appointed bishop of Guatemala in 1657 and took possession of his diocese in 1659. In 1668 he became archbishop of Mexico, and from 1674 to 1681 he served as viceroy. Interesting as Fray Payo's career is to the general historian, we can find time only to single out one short period of it, the winter of 1659, when he arrived in Guatemala. The aristocratic and learned prelate must have been gravely disappointed to discover there was no printing press in his see and, indeed, none save in Mexico City and Puebla de los Ángeles in all of Spanish North America.

Fray Payo immediately ascertained that there was an active desire to have a press in Guatemala, and he sent a Franciscan friar, Francisco de Borja, to Mexico City to procure a press and a printer. Early in 1660, perhaps in March, he was back in Guatemala with a printer, José de Pineda Ibarra, his family, a press, and a good assortment of type. Pineda Ibarra, a native of Mexico City and at one time an employee of the famous house of Calderón, had probably never been the proprietor of his own shop, and it was a step upward for him to move south to Guatemala. In 1660 the new printer managed to produce three rather slight pieces of which we have a record. Medina accords the honor of number one in his list to Fray Francisco de Quiñones y Escobedo's Sermon preached on 4 October 1660. For 1661 we have no recorded Guatemalan imprint, but for 1663 we have two small pieces and Fray Payo de Ribera's monumental Explicatio apologetica nonnullarum propositionum a theologo quodam non dextere notatarum, a work of 710 pages on which Pineda Ibarra must have been working since his first arrival.

The Explicatio and the Dominican Fr. Diego Sáenz Ovecuri's Thomasiada (1667), an epic poem of genuine merit, are Pineda Ibarra's two principal works. He continued to print at a fairly steady pace until 1679. After Pineda Ibarra's death in 1680, his son, Antonio de Pineda Ibarra, who had been born in Guatemala in 1661, took over the press and operated it at the same leisurely pace from 1681 to 1721. He was the only printer in Guatemala until 1714.

Among other early eighteenth century presses in Guatemala we might note those of the Franciscans (1714-1771),

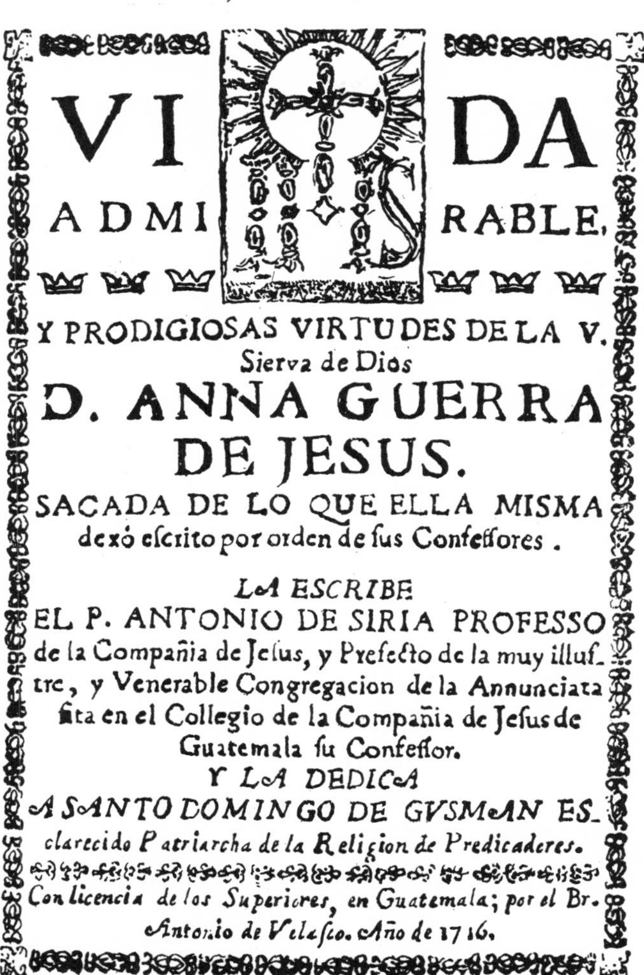

VI DA
ADMI RABLE,
Y PRODIGIOSAS VIRTUDES DE LA V.
Sierva de Dios
D. ANNA GUERRA
DE JESUS.
SACADA DE LO QUE ELLA MISMA
dexó eſcrito por orden de ſus Confeſſores.
LA ESCRIBE
EL P. ANTONIO DE SIRIA PROFESSO
de la Compañia de Jeſus, y Prefecto de la muy illuſ-
tre, y Venerable Congregacion de la Annunciata
ſita en el Collegio de la Compañia de Jeſus de
Guatemala ſu Confeſſor.
Y LA DEDICA
A SANTO DOMINGO DE GUSMAN ES-
clarecido Patriarcha de la Religion de Predicaderes.
Con licencia de los Superiores, en Guatemala; por el Br.
Antonio de Velaſco. Año de 1716.

Title-page of life of Ana Guerra printed in Guatemala by Antonio Velasco in 1716.

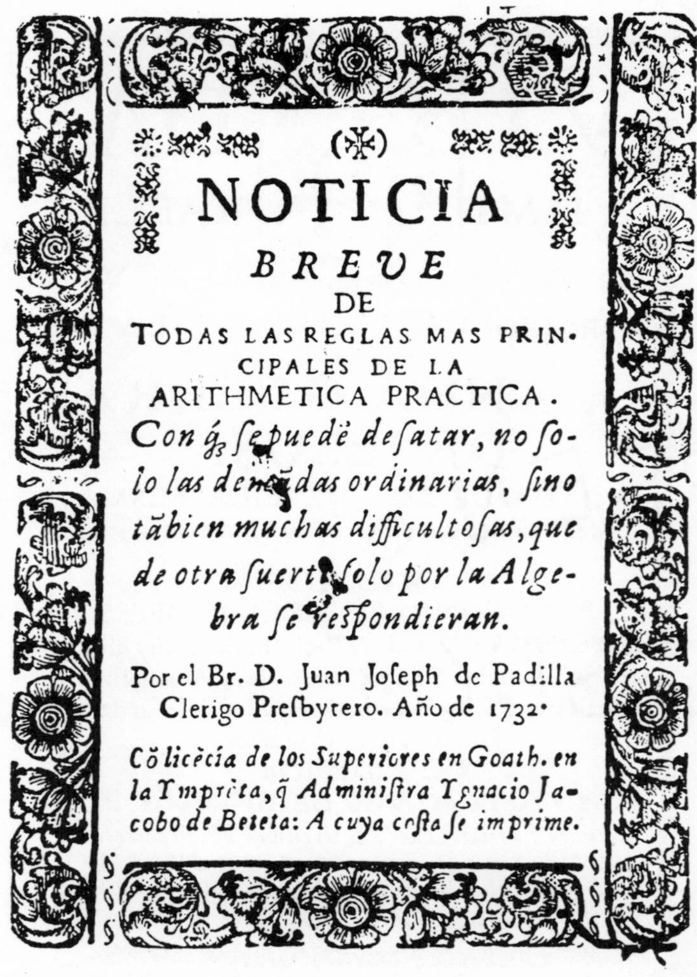

NOTICIA

BREVE

DE

TODAS LAS REGLAS MAS PRIN-
CIPALES DE LA
ARITHMETICA PRACTICA.

*Con q̃ ſe puedē deſatar, no ſo-
lo las demādas ordinarias, ſino
tābien muchas difficultoſas, que
de otra ſuerte ſolo por la Algebra ſe reſpondieran.*

Por el Br. D. Juan Joſeph de Padilla
Clerigo Preſbytero. Año de 1732.

*Cō licēcia de los Superiores en Goath. en
la Imprēta, q̃ Adminiſtra Ignacio Jacobo de Beteta: A cuya coſta ſe imprime.*

Title-page of an arithmetic printed in Guatemala in 1732 by Ignacio Jacobo de Beteta, the only known imprint from this minor press.

Antonio de Velasco (1715-1726), Sebastian de Arevalo (1727-1772), and above all, Cristóbal de Hincapié Meléndez (1739-1748), a native Guatemalan. Hincapié was a creative writer and a scientist as well as a printer and a picturesque personality in general. In all, Medina lists and describes the work of fourteen Guatemalan printers of the seventeenth and eighteenth centuries. The work of none is particularly distinguished from a typographical standpoint, and the volume of publication was relatively slight until the last two decades of the eighteenth century. Nevertheless, Guatemala was the second most important intellectual center of Spanish North America, and her leadership south of the Isthmus of Tehuantepec was maintained in cultural affairs even after independence was achieved, despite the bitter political rivalries in Central America in the nineteenth century.

Chapter VII

THE BEGINNING OF PRINTING IN NEW GRANADA

In the eighteenth century the viceroyalty of Nueva Granada included the presidency of Quito, the Audiencia of Santa Fé (de Bogotá), and the captaincy general and presidency of Caracas. This jurisdiction held together until after the wars of liberation. The break-up was natural, since the area is far from homogeneous; but royal authority maintained it in the colonial period, and therefore its printing history may be considered here in a single chapter.

Again in this jurisdiction there are uncertainties and obscure references which may conceivably lead to concrete discoveries in the future. The redoubtable Gonzalo Jiménez de Quesada, en route to find El Dorado, founded Santa Fé de Bogotá in 1538, and there is some evidence that the Franciscans or their friends were printing there before the end of the century. In the July-September, 1957, issue of the Revista Interamericana de Bibliografía Juan Friede cites a document in the Archivo de Indias which indicates that the Franciscan friar Pedro de Aguado sought permission to go to Nueva Granada to supervise the printing of his Historia del Nuevo Reino de Granada, since no books had been printed there before. On 5 February 1582 permission was granted, but the story ends here in a complete blank.

The first printing of which we have definite evidence in Bogotá is dated exactly two centuries after the foundation of the city. The Jesuits were responsible for the founding of the press, and here the first Bogotá imprint of which we have any record is Father Juan Ricaurte y Terreros, Septenario al corazón doloroso de María Santissima, with the imprint, "Con licencia. En Santa Fé de Bogotá: En la Imprenta de la Compañia de Jesus. Año de 1738". In his Bibliografía bogotana (1917) Eduardo Posada identifies ten imprints (one not located but known to have been printed) from this early Jesuit press between 1738 and 1742. The press served religious purposes exclusively, for eight of its nine surviving imprints are septenarios or novenas or similar publications, while the other deals with the privileges of the Jesuits. There is no record of the fate of the press after 1742, and it probably remained idle for a quarter of a century in the Jesuit house of San Bartolomé until all Jesuit property was secularized coincident with the expulsion.

The next notice of a printer in New Granada occurs in 1776, when we hear of a printer in Cartagena de Indias*, although we have no surviving product of any work he may have done in this community. In 1777 he was asked by the new viceroy to come to Bogotá, and in this year he produced an almanac. He was undoubtedly Antonio Espinosa de los Monteros, although he did not place his name on any of the books he published until 1782, when he already had fourteen titles to his credit. In this year he acquired a new press and new type from Cadiz and took the name of "Imprenta real". Printing thrived in Bogotá. In 1785 the first news-sheets appeared, and in 1791 a Papel periódico was founded. In 1793 Antonio Nariño set up a short-lived printing shop, "La Patriótica", under Diego Espinosa, son of Antonio, but this enterprise failed after Nariño was persecuted for his inflammatory Derechos del hombre (1793). The Imprenta real continued under Antonio Espinosa until 1804, when his son Bruno took it over. Once again, in 1810 "La Patriótica" appears as the name of a printing shop under Nicolás Calvo. Both the presses served political objectives of the revolutionaries, and Bruno Espinosa quite properly dropped the adjective real from his firm's name. New presses came in from the United States, and printing throve mightily in Colombia during the revolutionary decade.

*The first known Cartagena imprint is dated 1809. It is doubtful that anything was actually printed in Cartagena in 1776 or earlier.

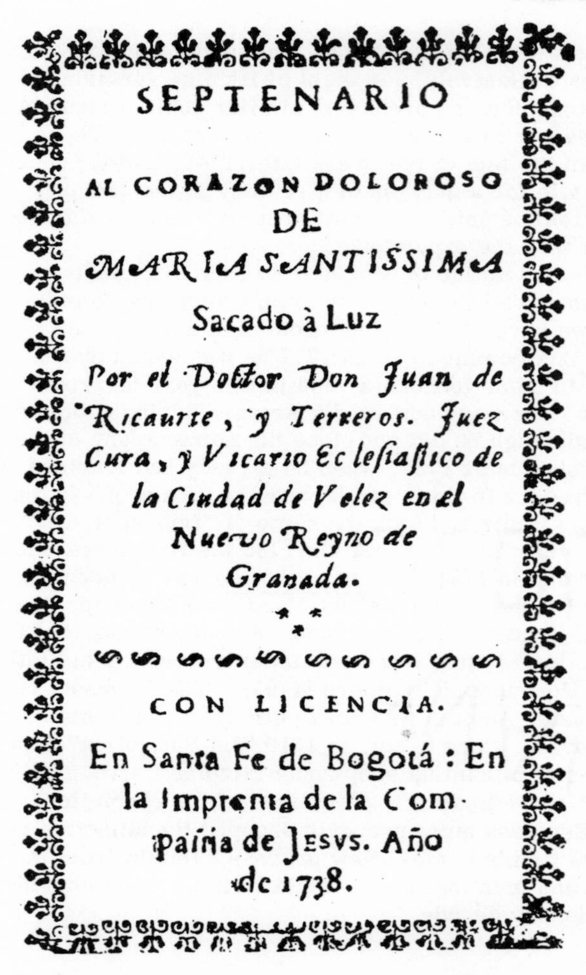
SEPTENARIO

AL CORAZON DOLOROSO
DE
MARIA SANTISSIMA

Sacado à Luz

Por el Doctor Don Juan de Ricaurte, y Terreros. Juez Cura, y Vicario Eclesiastico de la Ciudad de Velez en el Nuevo Reyno de Granada.

CON LICENCIA.

En Santa Fe de Bogotá: En la Imprenta de la Compañia de JESVS. Año de 1738.

Title-page of the Septenario printed by the Jesuits in Bogotá in 1738, the first surviving book printed in New Granada.

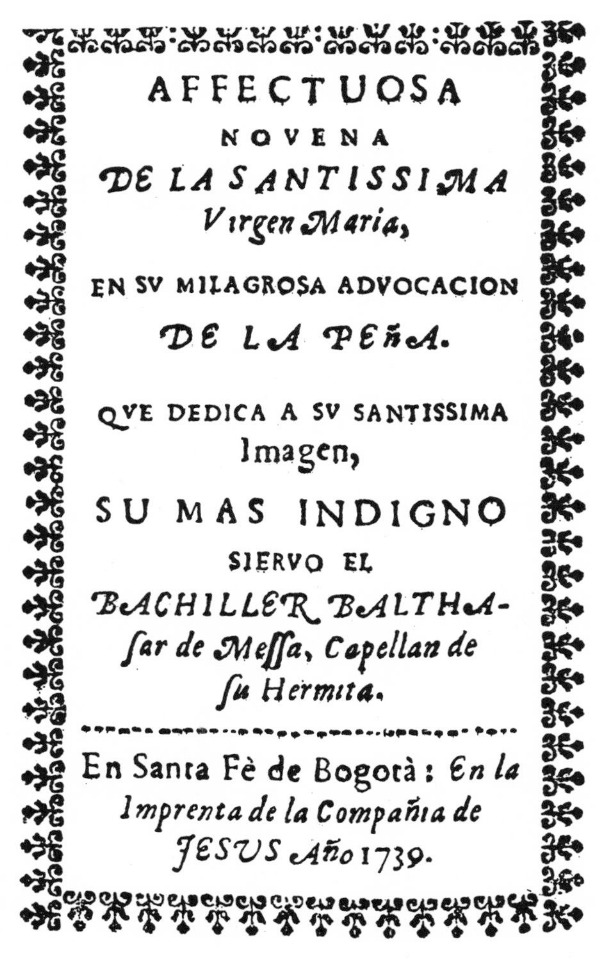

AFFECTUOSA
NOVENA
DE LA SANTISSIMA
Virgen Maria,
EN SV MILAGROSA ADVOCACION
DE LA PEñA.
QVE DEDICA A SV SANTISSIMA
Imagen,
SU MAS INDIGNO
SIERVO EL
BACHILLER BALTHA-
sar de Messa, Capellan de
su Hermita.

En Santa Fè de Bogotà: En la
Imprenta de la Compañia de
JESUS Año 1739.

Title-page of the Novena printed in Bogotá by the Jesuits in 1739, recorded by Enrique Posada as the second imprint of this city.

Thanks to the Historia de la imprenta en el Ecuador de 1755 a 1830 (1953), by Alexandre A. M. Stols, a Dutchman sent to Ecuador as a UNESCO expert, we have virtually all known information about early Ecuadorean printing gathered in one place. Stols lays several ghosts that have haunted even the pages of Medina's La imprenta en Quito, 1760-1818 (1904) and his Notas bibliográficas (1904), which described early printing in Ambato; but, above all, he provides straightforward, documented accounts and leaves few doubts about a story in which many points are obscure and subject to multiple interpretations.

Printing in Ecuador is another chapter in the triumphs and tragedies of the Company of Jesus in Latin America. As early as 1736-1740 the Jesuits tried to get a license to print from the Real Audiencia in Quito, but they had no success. In 1740 two prominent Ecuadorean Jesuits, José María Maugeri, a Sicilian by birth, and Tomás Nieto Polo del Aguila, a native of Popayán (Colombia) were sent to Europe with various objectives, one of which was to buy a press for the private use of their community. With them was one Alejandro Coronado, a poor copyist of Quito who worked for the Jesuit residence. We do not know all the details of what happened in Spain, but Stols makes the following very likely deductions: The two priests arranged for Coronado to secure a royal cédula from the Consejo de Indias, permitting him to operate a public printing office in Quito. Coronado, a man of humble circumstances, could not buy a press, but the Jesuits could; and their equipment, with Coronado's license, could permit the establishment of a public press. Unfortunately Coronado died in Spain, and his mother (Angela) in Quito inherited the rights granted by the cédula. The Jesuits then arranged for her to sign over the cédula to one Raimundo de Salazar. In the meanwhile, however, the press which the fathers bought or intended to buy did not reach Ecuador, and Salazar could do nothing. Sra. Angela Coronado revoked the earlier contract and turned over the cédula to the procurador of the Colegio Maximo of the Jesuits.

When and how a press reached Ecuador we do not know. When it did, it was set up in the new Jesuit college in Ambato, some seventy-five miles south of Quito. We do not know the exact reasons why it was located here. We may quess it was at the instigation of Father Maugeri, who was probably the moving spirit behind the importation of the press and who had founded the college at great personal sacrifice. The first printer was Juan Adán Schwartz, probably a native of Hamburg, who entered the Jesuit Order in 1751 and arrived in Quito in 1754. Schwartz' first production came in 1755, St. Bonaventure's Piisima erga Dei genetricem devotio, a substantial publication of ninety-two pages. In the next four years, until 1759, eleven other books and pamphlets, all of less than a hundred pages, appeared in Ambato. There is no evidence that a Catalogus personarum was printed in Ambato in 1754. This tale seems to derive from Pablo Herrera, a nineteenth century historian of Ecuador.

In 1759 Father Maugeri was transferred to Quito. Since he was the only person in Ambato who was concerned with matters of publication, his transfer was probably the reason that Schwartz and the press were moved to Quito. The first Quito imprint was again the work of a Jesuit, Juan Bautista Aguirre's Divino religionis propugnaculo polari fidelium syderi (1759). Subsequently fifteen other publications, nearly all religious in content, appeared from Schwartz' press. In 1767 the Jesuits were expelled from South America, and Schwartz was jammed into the hold of a Panama-bound ship in Guayaquil with a cargo of disease-ridden Negroes. He, like hundreds of other Jesuits in both hemispheres, died as a result of the brutal conditions of expulsion. Schwartz was a competent designer and a good pressman, qualities continued in the work of his successor, Raimundo de Salazar, who printed in Quito from 1767 to 1793, after the government took over Jesuit property. Indeed, no other colonial Latin American press did better work in this period. After Salazar stopped printing in 1794, Mauricio de los Reyes succeeded him as Quito's printer, but his work was distinctly inferior

PIISSIMA
ERGA
DEI GENITRICEM
DEVOTIO
Ad impetrandam gratiam
pro articulo mortis.
Ex Seraphico Doctore Divo
Bonaventura deprompta.
Cura, & solicitudine servorum
JEsu, Mariæ, & Joseph.
Cum variis Orationibus ante, &
post Confession. & Commun.
Cum Licentia.

HAMBATI,
Typis, Soc. JEsu. Anno 1755.

Title-page of St. Bonaventure's Piisima erga Dei genetricem devotio (Ambato, 1755), the first known Ecuadorean imprint.

LA ESCLAVITUD
MAS HONROSA
EXERCICIO
QUE CADA DIA PUEDEN
practicar los devotos Esclavos
EN OBSEQUIO
DE LA GRAN REYNA
DE CIELOS, Y TIERRA
MARIA SS.MA
DEL CARMEN.
A mayor Gloria de Dios,
Honra de tan Gran Madre, Consuelo, y provecho de las
Almas.

HAMBATI, typis Soc JESU
Anni 1759.

Title-page of a book printed in 1759, the last year of the Jesuit press in Ambato.

PONTIFICALE
ROMANUM
CLEMENTIS VIII. primum,
nunc denuò
URBANI PAPÆ VIII.
AUTHORITATE RECOGNITUM
CLEMENTIS
PAPÆ VIII.
CONSTITUTIO
Super Pontificalis Editionem.
Cum Facultate Superiorum.

HAMBATI . typis Societatis JEsu.
Anno 1755.

Title-page of the second Ambato imprint of 1755.

to that of his two predecessors. He was succeeded by José Mauricio de los Reyes and Miguel de los Reyes, who printed from 1797 to 1799 and from 1801 to 1810, respectively, but their products are few, their biographies obscure.

Medina maintained stoutly that José Luís de Cisneros, Descripción exacta de la Provincia de Benezuela, "Impreso en Valencia, Año de M.DCC. LXIV", was actually printed in 1764 in Nueva Valencia, Venezuela. Don Pedro Grases, a Spaniard who has become the recognized dean of Venezuelan bibliographers, differs with this view; and in two articles in the Revista Nacional de Cultura for 1947 and 1949 respectively, he argues rather convincingly that this book was actually printed in San Sebastian, Spain, by Riesgo y Montero, printers to the Compañia Guipuzcoana. It seems most likely that printing did not come to Nueva Valencia until Juan Gutiérrez set up his shop there in 1812.

There have also been some differences of opinion about the introduction of printing in Caracas, but both Grases and Medina agree that the first Caracas imprint was the Gaceta de Caracas for 24 October 1808. The printers were Mateo Gallagher and Jaime Lamb, both North Americans; and their press had originally been brought to Venezuelan shores by the expeditionary fleet of General Francisco Miranda when he attacked the province of Coro. Evidently Miranda could not use it but left it in Trinidad, where Gallagher and Lamb acquired it. Printing had been introduced to Port-of-Spain, Trinidad, on 11 August 1786 by Juan Cassan, who printed an Ordenanza. However, Trinidad was lost to Spain in 1802 and has since been English in all its traditions.

Printing flourished in Venezuela after its introduction. In 1810 Gallagher and Lamb published the first non-serial Caracas imprint, the Calendario manual, y guía universal de forasteros, of which Grases brought out a facsimile in 1952. Printing came to Cumaná in 1811; to Nueva Valencia, as already noted, in 1812; to Angostura (Ciudad Bolívar) in 1819; and to Maracaibo and Puerto Cabello in 1822.

)(✠)(

DESCRIPCION EXACTA DE LA PROVINCIA DE BENEZUELA,

POR

D. JOSEPH LUIS DE CISNEROS.

DEDICALA

A UN INCOGNITO AMIGO SUYO.

....

IMPRESSO EN VALENCIA,

Año de M. DCCLXIV.

Title-page of the much debated description of Venezuela by José Luís de Cisneros, said by Medina to have been printed in Nueva Valencia, Venezuela, in 1764.

CALENDARIO MANUAL,

Y

GUIA UNIVERSAL DE FORASTEROS

EN

VENEZUELA,

PARA EL AÑO DE

1810.

Con Superior Permiso.

Muy Curioso.

CARACAS:

EN LA IMPRENTA DE GALLAGHER Y LAMB.

One of the oldest specimens of [illegible] printing in Caracas and very rare.

Title-page of the first non-serial Caracas imprint, the Calendario manual of 1810.

Chapter VIII

THE BEGINNING OF PRINTING IN CHILE

The origin of printing in Chile was long clouded in mystery, and even Medina was unaware of the real facts when he compiled La Imprenta en Santiago (1891). Today it is generally accepted that the first press was brought to Chile by an aristocratic German Jesuit, Carlos Haimhausen. According to Domingo Amunategui Solar's account of the beginnings of printing in Chile in the Revista Chilena de Historia y Geografía for 1933, Father Haimhausen was sent to Spain as the procurador for the provincial congregation of Chile. He organized a missionary team of some forty individuals, many of them skilled artisans; and, what is more important, he acquired large stocks of supplies and equipment to promote trade and industry in Chile, up to that time primarily a colony of farmers and frontier fighters. When Haimhausen arrived in Buenos Aires in November 1747, he had his shipments checked by the officers of the captain-general of Buenos Aires, Don José de Adonaegui. The records show that the customs agents in Buenos Aires found "cinco cajones para imprenta de libros" among Haimhausen's 386 boxes and bundles; and we also know that royal officials in Santiago checked in these five boxes on 6 May 1748.

Most of Haimhausen's group was settled on the hacienda of Calera de Tango with their equipment, but the press and the type were sent to the Universidad de San Felipe. We do not know whether it was used for printing prior to Haimhausen's death in May 1767 and the Jesuit expulsion four months later. At least nothing from this period of the press has been discovered. The first surviving Chilean imprint that has come down to us is the Modo de ganar el jubileo santo (1776), a slender pamphlet of nine pages, extremely poorly printed. An unsatisfactory facsimile was published in 1910 by Ramón A. Laval under the title of Un incunable chileno. It was taken from the one surviving copy bound in a pamphlet volume once in the collection of Ramón Briseño and now in the Biblioteca Nacional in Santiago. This copy is in bad condition; and this factor, combined with the poor halftones, make the facsimile illegible in many places. We know nothing about the printer or the conditions of printing; but there is no evidence that there was any press in Chile in 1776 other than the one imported by Father Haimhausen a quarter of a century earlier.

Medina records twenty-one pieces, mainly broadsides of an official character, printed in Santiago between 1780 and 1811; but in spite of Laval's discovery his assertion that Chile had no proper press during the colonial period is essentially correct. Chilean writers were compelled to send their manuscripts of books to the peninsula to be published. The noted Bishop Gaspar de Villaroel entrusted to a certain person some manuscripts and a substantial sum from his poor box for printing costs. The manuscripts were lost, and the agent embezzled the funds. Such was the problem that many a creative writer in Chile and, indeed, in other places throughout the Indies, faced when he aspired to break into print.

It seems most likely that the Santiago imprints recorded by Medina were printed on Haimhausen's press, but only fragmentary information is available about the printers and the circumstances of printing. We know that there was a press (probably Haimhausen's) in the University. José Camilo Gallardo, warden (bedel) of the University, mastered printing in a desultory fashion and produced some of the invitations and offical announcements recorded in Medina's list of 1780-1811 imprints. However, neither Gallardo nor anyone else who may have operated the Haimhausen press printed any work necessitating a sustained effort.

In 1790 the Cabildo of Santiago de Chile had requested permission from the king to establish a regular printing shop, but nothing came of the project.

As late as 1803 it was necessary to have a Reglamento del hospicio de pobres de la ciudad de Santiago printed in

✠

HESPERIAE

MONARCHÆ

INDIARUMQUE IMPERATORI.

Publicæ Tranquilitatis Auctori.
CAROLO, inquam nomine III.
Scientiarum MECOENATI.
Hosce ribulos ex Fontibus Theologiæ de
promptos. Per Manus.
EXmi D.D. AUGUSTINI à JAUREGUI, Dignissimi Chilensis Regni
Supremi Ducis &c. &c.

V. D. O. C. Q.

D. Josephus Ignacius Gutierrez, Regij
Collegij Carolini Alumnus
ópem ferente
D. Michaele Josepho de Lastarria, ejusdem
Convictorij Magistro.

Title-page of a short religious disputation printed in Santiago de Chile in 1780.

DIRECTORIUM.

AD HORAS CANONICAS PERsolvendas, Missasque celebrandas juxta Ritum Sanctæ Romanæ Ecclesiæ, nec no: Rubricas Breviarii, et Missalis Romani. Ad ussum, et commoditatem Cleri sæcularis Civitatis Sancti Jacobi de Chile.

DISPOSITUM, ET ORDINATUM,

A D. EMANUELE CAIETANO de Medina Ecclesiæ Collegii maximi Sancti Michaelis Archangeli Capellano.

Pro Anno Dñi 1800.

Este Directorio se hallara en el Alma cen de D. Ignacio Landa,

Title-page of a religious calendar printed in Santiago de Chile by José Camilo Gallardo in 1800.

DIRECTORIUM

PRO DIUINO OFFICIO PERSOL-
vendo, Sacroque Missæ Sacrificio cele-
brando juxta Kitum Sanctæ Romanæ
Ecclesiæ, nec non Rubricas Breviarii, &
Missalis Romani Ad usum, & commo
ditatèm Cleri Secularis Civitatis Sancti
Jacobi de Chile.

DISPOSITUM, ET ORDINATUM

A D. EMMANUELE CAIETANO
de Medina Ecclesiæ Colegii Sancti Mi
chaelis Archangeli Capellano.

Pro Anno Dni. 1801.

Typis Camili Gallardo.

Este Directorio se hallara en el Almacen
de D. Ignacio Landa.

Title-page of a religious directory printed in Santiago de Chile by José Camilo Gallardo in 1801.

Buenos Aires. When the struggle for Chilean independence formally began on 18 September 1810, it was clear that the absence of an effective printing shop could no longer be tolerated. A native of Gothenburg, whose name is recorded in Chilean history as Mateo Arnaldo Hoevel (Havel)*, deserves a large measure of credit for bringing a regular press to Chile. With the cooperation of John R. Livingston of New York, Hoevel brought a press and three North American printers (Samuel Burr Johnston, William H. Burbidge, and Simon Garrison). He received 6,389 pesos from the government for the press, the cost of installation, and for various small arms that arrived with the press. On 13 February 1812 the Yankee printers produced the first issue of the Aurora de Chile, a weekly under the editorship of Fray Camilo Henríquez and over the imprint of "este Superior Gobierno". The last issue of the Aurora appeared on 1 April 1813. A new newspaper El Monitor Araucano, began publication on 6 April 1813 "En la Imprenta de Gobierno P.D.J.C. Gallardo". Three months later, on 29 June, Gallardo rented the press from the government and continued to hold it through the Spanish occupation (1814-1817). The Monitor ceased publication on 1 October 1814, and Gallardo, a royalist at heart, quickly found a modus vivendi with the new masters of Santiago. However, when the forces of San Martín and O'Higgins swept into northern Chile, Gallardo was stigmatized "por ser un individuo contrario al sistema"; and the burden of maintaining Chile's typographical traditions passed to other hands.

*1773-1819, the first foreigner to earn Chilean citizenship (1811), mayor of Santiago (1817), and founder of a distinguished Chilean family.

AURORA DE CHILE
PERIODICO
MINISTERIAL, Y POLITICO.

VIVA LA UNION, LA PATRIA, Y EL REY.

PROSPECTO.

ESTÁ ya en nuestro poder, el grande, el presioso instrumento de la ilustracion universal, la Imprenta.

Mas ya por un beneficio de la Providencia digno de nuestra eterna gratitud, despertamos de aquel letargo profundo, y hemos tomado un movimiento grande, é

Aurora
DE
CHILE,
PERIODICO
MINISTERIAL, Y POLITICO.

Tomo Primero....Año de 1812.

SANTIAGO DE CHILE:

En la Imprenta de este Superior Gobierno.

CON SUPERIOR PERMISO,
IMPRESO EN SANTIAGO DE CHILE,
EN LA IMPRENTA DE ESTE SUPERIOR GOBIERNO,
POR SRES. SAMUEL B. JOHNSTON, GUILLELMO H. BURBIDGE, Y SIMON GARRISON,
DE LOS ESTADOS UNIDOS.

Año de 1812.

The weekly Aurora de Chile was printed by North Americans and edited by Camilo Henríquez.

Chapter IX

THE BEGINNING OF PRINTING IN THE SPANISH ANTILLES

One might normally have assumed that printing would have followed the course of the empire in Spanish America and found its first home in the Antilles. In reality the oldest settlements were among the most backward in acquiring presses. Santo Domingo and Panamá knew nothing of printing before the nineteenth century. It was not until 1807 that so ancient a Caribbean community as San Juan de Puerto Rico acquired a press. In the British Antilles and even in British Guiana printing was well established in the eighteenth century, especially in Jamaica and Barbados. Life was perhaps a bit too easy in most of the islands to stimulate the cultivation of European crafts.

An exception was Cuba, the seat of a captain general and always the richest and most significant of the islands. The beginning of printing in Cuba has been clouded by unfounded rumor and slipshod research to which even such distinguished bibliographers as Beristain de Souza and Antonio Bachiller y Morales have contributed. The first Cuban printer of whom we may speak with any certainty was Carlos Habré, a foreigner, probably a Frenchman, of whom we know almost nothing. His first known imprint is a _Tarifa general de precios de medicina_ (Havana, 1723), reprinted in facsimile by Manuel Pérez Beato in his _La primera obra impresa en Cuba_ (1936). The only other two books from Habré's press that we know for certain are the _Méritos que ha justificado y probado el Ldo. D. Antonio de Sossa_ (1724) and the _Rúbricas generales generales del breviario romano_ (1727). Until further proof is presented, we cannot accept any other Cuban imprints rumored to have existed before 1736.

We know little more about the life and work of Cuba's second printer, Francisco José de Paula. On 4 June 1735 the Cabildo in Havana approved the issuance of a license to de Paula to print, possibly a recognition of the need of the new University of Havana (founded in 1734) for a printer. The first product of de Paula's press was, in fact, a university thesis by Juan Bautista Sollozo y Urrea, Coelestis astrea (1736). Only two other publications of de Paula's are known, another thesis and an Ordo recitandi officium divinum, both dated 1741. We know that de Paula received an appointment as printer to the Tribunal de Cruzada in 1741, and Bachiller says that de Paula sold his shop to Manuel Azpeitia, from whom it later passed to Esteban José Boloña.

The third printer in Havana was Blas de los Olivos, whose first imprint was a broadside entitled Receta facil y provechosa contra dolores y llagas provenidas de humor galico (1757), formerly in the British Museum but destroyed by enemy action in World War II. Blas de los Olivos' last imprint is dated 1777, and there are barely a dozen publications which may be definitely attributed to his press during its two decades of activity. Count Ricla attempted to make arrangements with Blas de los Olivos to print a "Gazeta", a "Mercurio mensual", and a "Guía de forasteros" with an almanac, but Madrid frowned on the project. Indeed, on 20 January 1777 there was issued a royal cédula stating, "There shall be no printing house in the island, now or in the future, other than that of the Captaincy General". Fortunately, this cédula never took effect, thanks to a succession of liberal governors, notably General Luis de las Casas, in the 1790's.

The printing house of the Cómputo eclesiástico began to serve the Cathedral and the various religious orders in 1762. From 1776 until the end of the century it used the more descriptive title of "Imprenta de la Curia Episcopal y Colegio Seminario de San Carlos". Its publications are, naturally, on religious themes.

In 1781 the "Imprenta de la Capitanía General" began to function with the publication of a Guía de forasteros and was the main printing house of Havana for the next three decades. In 1782 this shop began to issue the Gazeta de la Habana, first under Diego de la Barrera and later under Francisco Seguí,

ORACION FUNEBRE
DEL EXMO. SEñOR BAYLIO
FREY D. ANTONIO
MARIA BUCARELI, Y URSUA, HENES-trosa, Lazo de la Vega, Villacis, y Cordova: Caballero Gran Cruz, y Comendador de la Tocina en el Orden de San Juan, Gentil Hombre de Camara de S. M. con entrada, Teniente General de los Reales Exercitos, Virrey, Gobernador, y Capitan General del Reyno de Nueva España, Presidente de su Real Audiencia, Superintendente General de Real Hacienda, y Ramo del Tabaco, Juez Conservador de este, Presidente de su Junta, y Subdelegado de la Renta de Correos en el mismo Reyno.

QVE DIXO

EL DOCTOR DON JUAN GARCIA BARRERAS PRESBYtero, Calificador del Santo Oficio, Cathedratico del Angelico Dor. Sto. Thomas en la Real, y Pontificia Universidad de S. Geronimo, el Primero de Sagrada Theologia en el Real Seminario de San Carlos por S. M. Director Interino del proprio Colegio por el Illmo. Sr. Obispo de Cuba, Consultor Theologo de Camara de su S. Illma, Secretario del Segundo Concilio Diocesano, y Examinador Synodal del Obispado, En la Iglesia Parroquial mayor de S. Christoval de esta Ciudad de la Havana el dia 2 de Junio de 1779

CON LAS LICENCIAS NECESARIAS
En la Havana en la Imprenta de la Curia Eclesiastica y Real Seminario de San Carlos.

Title-page of Barreras' Oración funebre del exmo. Señor Baylio Frey D. Antonio María Bucareli, 1779.

who was associated in some way with the family of Blas de los Olivos.

In 1787 Esteban José de Boloña initiated an important printing tradition in Havana when he began to print Ignacio José de Urrutia Montoya's Teatro histórico jurídico, político militar de la Isla Fernandina de Cuba. This promising work ceased after the appearance of the first fascicle, but Urrutia's notes were undoubtedly used for his important Compendio de memorias published by the Imprenta de la Capitanía General. Despite his initial fragmentary effort, Boloña (whose relation to the alleged purchaser of de Paula's press we know not) thrived, and he and his descendants were prominent printers in Havana until the middle of the nineteenth century. Boloña laid a sound foundation for the prosperity of his firm by securing official affiliation with the Inquisition in 1792 and the title of printer to the Royal Navy, in 1793. The imprints of the Boloña family were distinguished both for design and typography.

The last Havana printer who should be mentioned is Pedro Palma (or Pedro Palmé or Pedro Nolasco Palmer), a sergeant invalided out of the army after two decades of service. He was first denied permission to print in view of the royal cédula of 1777, but the enlightened Governor Las Casas supported his request so vigorously that he was given permission to open his shop in 1791.

In 1790 the Imprenta de la Capitanía General began to issue the noteworthy Papel periódico de la Habana, the first bonafide magazine in Cuba. It was a major force in the intellectual life of the Habaneros for two decades and it was later known as El aviso and Diario de la Habana.

The history of Cuba in the nineteenth century bears out only in part the bright promise of late eighteenth century Cuban publishing. The liberal governors of the period around the turn of the century were succeeded by small-minded men determined to hang on to Spain's last foothold in the western hemisphere at any cost. It was with the greatest difficulty that Cuban patriots were able to communicate effectively to

DESCRIPCION
DE DIFERENTES PIEZAS
DE HISTORIA NATURAL
LAS MAS
DEL RAMO MARITIMO,
REPRESENTADAS
EN SETENTA Y CINCO LAMINAS.

SU AUTOR
Don Antonio Parra.

EN LA HAVANA AÑO DE 1787.

CON LAS LICENCIAS NECESARIAS.
En la Imprenta de la Capitania General.

Title-page of Antonio Parra's *Descripción de diferentes piezas de historia natural*, issued in 1787 by the Imprenta de la Capitanía General, from original in John Carter Brown Library.

GRACIA CONCEDIDA

POR S. M.

Á LOS HABITANTES DE ESTA ISLA

PARA

LA INTRODUCCION DE CABALLOS

frisones de ambos sexôs, desde las

Provincias del Norte de América.

En Real Orden de 9 de Junio

de 1798.

HAVANA:

En la Imprenta de la Capitanía General.

Publication of Imprenta de la Capitanía (Library of Congress duplicate, now in University of Kentucky Library) recording the origins of a great sports relationship in the Americas.

ESTATUTOS

DE LA

SOCIEDAD PATRIOTICA

DE LA HAVANA

APROBADOS POR S. M.

AÑO  DE 1793.

CON LICENCIA.

EN LA HAVANA

En la Imprenta de la Capitanía General.

Title-page of a fundamental document of an organization that was a major force in Cuban literary, bibliographical and library history until the late 1950's. Original in University of Kentucky.

fellow-countrymen; but men such as Blas de los Olivos, Las Casas, and Boloña had nevertheless established an ineradicable tradition of a strong (although not free) press which was to be of the greatest inspiration to Cuban patriots in the culmination of events in the 1890's.

Note: The strained political relationships between Cuba and the United States in 1962 have created a barrier in communications between individuals residing or formerly residing in these jurisdictions. For this reason it has not been possible to secure photographic copies of title-pages of certain early Cuban imprints which were inspected by the writer in private and public libraries in Cuba in 1956 and 1957.

INDEX